IMAGES
of America

MADISON

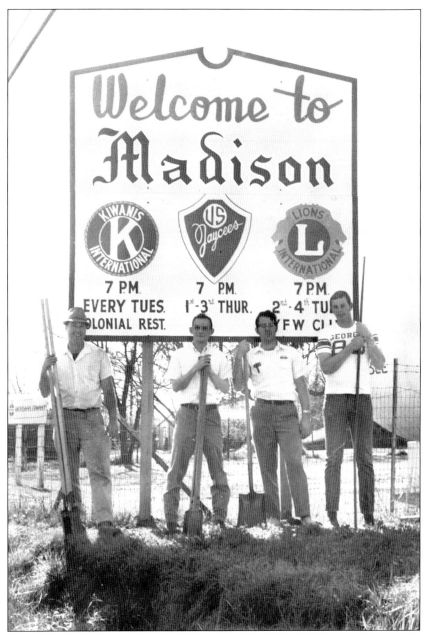

Welcome to Madison! (Courtesy of the Morgan County Archives.)

ON THE COVER: Members of Madison Baptist Church Sunday school are pictured in 1912 in front of the church. This photograph was taken prior to the addition of a front portico and columns. The church is just south of the town square, at the corner of South Main Street and Central Avenue. The church was built with bricks made by slaves on the Morgan County plantation of John Byne Walker, one of the early parishioners. According to legend, Union horses were stabled in the church basement during the Civil War. (Courtesy of Morgan County Heritage website.)

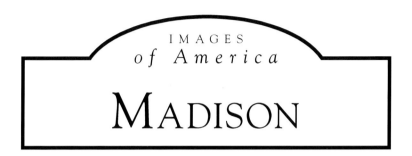

IMAGES
of America

MADISON

Marcia Brooks and Kittie Mayfield

ARCADIA
PUBLISHING

Published by Arcadia Publishing
Charleston, South Carolina

Printed in the United States of America

Library of Congress Control Number: 2012934592

For all general information, please contact Arcadia Publishing:
Telephone 843-853-2070
Fax 843-853-0044
E-mail sales@arcadiapublishing.com
For customer service and orders:
Toll-Free 1-888-313-2665

Visit us on the Internet at www.arcadiapublishing.com

This book is dedicated to all those who have called Madison their home through the years. This is their story.

CONTENTS

ACKNOWLEDGMENTS

The authors owe a deep measure of gratitude to the following individuals and organizations for their assistance in compiling this book: Tara Cooner, secretary of Morgan County Resource Preservation Advisory Board; Stratton Hicky for generous use of his personal photographs and knowledge; Carol Cross for information provided; Connie Shatterly Malone for providing photographs; Tim Lavelle at Morgan County High School for access to photographs of Madison A&M; Morgan County Library and branch manager Miriam Baker for use of research materials and photographs and library assistant Penny West for a wealth of details and background information; director Mamie Hillman and staff of the Morgan County African American Museum for information and authorization to use photographs; City of Madison manager David Nunn and City of Madison Water Department manager Larry Stephens for information; Monoray Powers of the *Morgan County Citizen* weekly newspaper for information; Bank of Madison CEO Clifton Hanes for information; and our editors at Arcadia Publishing, Elizabeth Bray and Jeff Ruetsche, for their guidance and assistance.

   And last, but not least, a special word of thanks to the Morgan County Archives and director Marshall "Woody" Williams for use of the facility and photographs and for sharing his vast knowledge of the area and also to archivist Linda Williams.

INTRODUCTION

The humble origins of Madison, Georgia, can be traced to the area near Calvary Baptist Church on Academy Street, known for its cool spring water. A settlement was located here prior to the town's incorporation in 1809. The town was named for the nation's newly elected president, James Madison. It became the county seat of Morgan County, which had been incorporated in 1807.

Madison's location placed it on a main east-west stagecoach route. In the early 1800s, the town bustled with travelers. It became a popular stop on the route. In the 1845 *Guide to Georgia*, Madison was called "the most cultured and aristocratic town on the stagecoach route from Charleston to New Orleans." Several taverns were located in town to accommodate travelers. One of those taverns, known as the Stagecoach House, still stands on Old Post Road.

The railroad came to Madison in the late 1830s. Travel and movement of goods by rail was much faster than by stagecoach and afforded travelers shelter from the elements. For a time, Madison was the terminus of the Georgia Railroad. Residents from the village of Marthasville rode out to Madison by horseback once per week to pick up mail, until the tracks were extended westward, eventually reaching the new city of Atlanta (formerly Marthasville) and beyond. The railroad played a pivotal role in the development of Madison and many other towns in Georgia. It also practically eliminated stagecoach travel.

Although best known for its Temple Greek antebellum architecture, the vast majority of Madison's historic homes were built in a variety of other styles, including Victorian, front gable side-wing, cottage, Federal, and various combinations. The historic district in Madison is the second largest in the state of Georgia. Only Macon's is larger. Some of the homes have been maintained for generations by single families, but Madison was also an early champion of historic preservation, one of the major reasons the town is so well preserved and pristine today.

The business district of Madison grew southward from the rails, which roughly paralleled the earlier stagecoach route that ran along still earlier Native American trails. The town square was laid out two blocks south of the route, and the streets surrounding the square were originally named for American presidents. Morgan County's first courthouse stood on the square. Begun in 1808, it was completed 15 years later but was lost to fire in 1844. Soon, a second courthouse was built in the same location. In 1907, the county decided to build a new courthouse one block south of the square. The old courthouse stood on the square until 1916, when fire destroyed it as well. Madison's US Post Office stands on this location today.

Though spared Sherman's torch for the most part, several of the town's businesses have experienced fires over the years, the worst by far in 1869. Early town buildings were constructed of wood. In 1869, a fire started in one of the town's businesses, and it soon spread to other buildings and became a firestorm. Few of the town's early downtown buildings survived the conflagration. As a result of this disaster, businesses were eventually rebuilt of brick masonry. Many of these buildings still stand today along the downtown streets.

With the railroad came people and the need for schools. Throughout the second half of the 19th century, Madison became well known as a center of education. Several academies were located in Madison during this time, and a few of the buildings from that era still stand. Several noteworthy individuals were associated with the academies. Alexander Hamilton Stephens taught in one of the academies in his early 20s. Rebecca Latimer Felton was a graduate of one of the academies.

Although Madison is well known for its homes being spared during Sherman's March to the Sea, the residents of Madison experienced hardships during the Civil War just like those in other towns in Georgia. At the Stokes-McHenry home, Madison resident James Smith died after being shot by drunken Union soldiers during an argument. Animals and valuables were taken by the Union troops, and they left their calling card at the railroad tracks, twisting the rails into useless straps of metal. Many citizens found themselves reverting back to stagecoaches temporarily to get around.

The dawn of the 20th century brought with it the promise of many technological advancements. Water and power had come to the town in the 1890s, and it was not long before the automobile made its debut in Madison. But Morgan County was, and still is, primarily a rural area. Agriculture has always been an integral part of the economy for its citizens, including those in the town. Farmers from the surrounding county areas came to Madison to conduct their business, and they came on horseback or by wagon. Several livery stables conducted business in Madison up until the 1930s and 1940s.

Gradually the county, and the town, modernized. Madison's first airport was built in the 1930s by the Works Progress Administration (WPA) on land later occupied by Wellington Puritan Mills, Inc. Several plants brought industry to the area during the 20th century. In the 1960s, Interstate 20 came to Madison, and a second business district grew around the US Highway 441 interchange about three miles south of the square. A new airport north of town was completed in the 1970s, and Madison has continued to grow.

But even with this growth, Madison has not lost its small-town charm. Walking along the quiet, shady streets of the historic district gives one the feeling of walking into history. Despite its prominence in tourism, Madison has not lost its authenticity, its "realness." And this is the true beauty of Madison.

One

THE PEOPLE OF MADISON

Most of the people in this chapter are not famous. They are friends, coworkers, and relatives living their everyday lives. Each one has made their mark on Madison in a unique and special way. Some were business leaders. Some were heavily involved in civic activities. Some gave to the town through acts of devotion or philanthropy. And others were just hardworking, unassuming, simple people who have played a part in the history of Madison. They have shared tragedies and triumphs, and through it all, they have taken care of the town for over 200 years, ensuring that new generations would have the opportunity to live in or visit an authentic Southern town.

More than anything else, the people of Madison have carefully planned the future of the town, ensuring that new development is consistent with its ideals and preserves the town's character. If not for the people of Madison, it would not be the Madison known and loved today. In 2009, the people of Madison celebrated the bicentennial anniversary of its incorporation and now look forward to what the future will bring. The people of Madison are its soul.

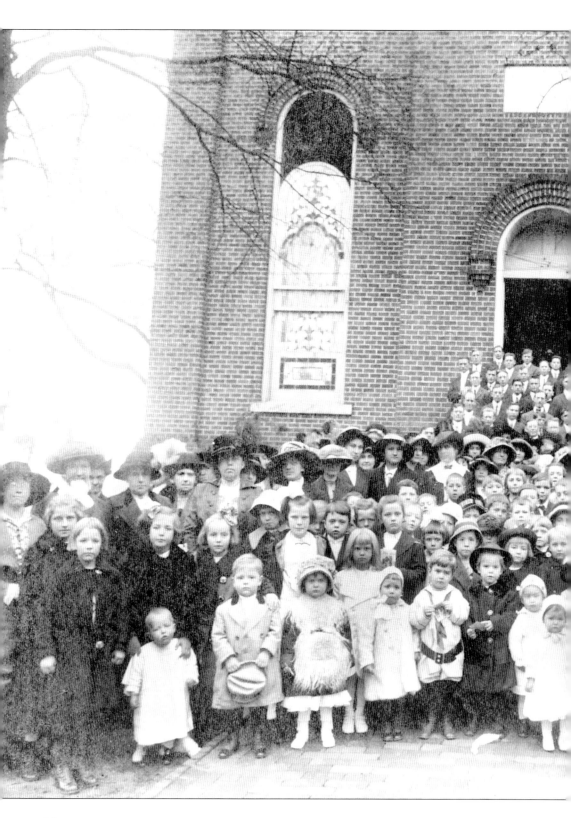

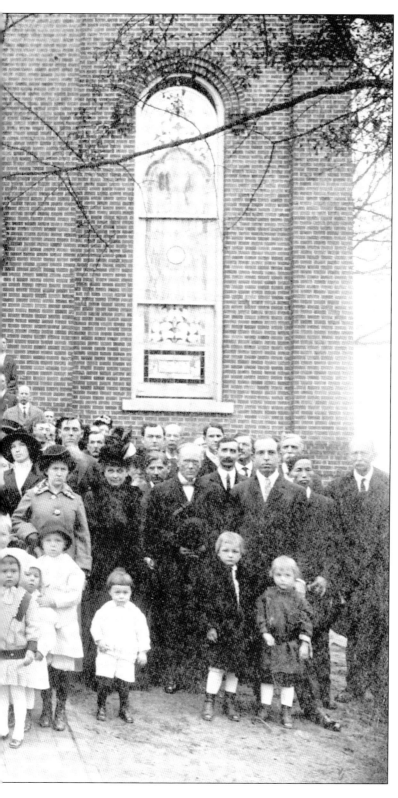

Members of Madison Baptist Church Sunday school are pictured in 1912 in front of the church. The following have been identified in this picture: Sara Brady, Rossar Zachary, Mary Stokes, R.N. Kimbrough, Harris Shouse, Lal Penick, J.H. Hunter, Q.L. and Frances Baldwin Williford, Robert Harris, Andrew Torbert, Mary Louise Torbert Chiles, Janet Torbert, Julian Foster, Newton Thompson, Mrs. Ralph Rish, Richter Waters, Mrs. May Niles, Mason Williams, Grady Wilson, and Loo Lee. (Courtesy of Morgan County Heritage website.)

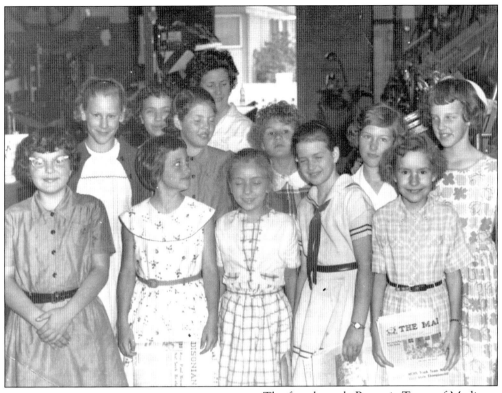

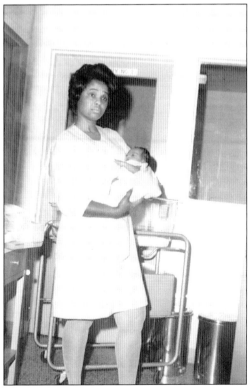

The fourth grade Brownie Troop of Madison is shown during its visit to the *Madisonian* printing plant in May 1960. Pictured are, from left to right, (first row) Connie James, Joan Norton, Cindy Hawk, Mary Jo Ainslie, and Winkie Vaughn; (second row) Judy Walker, Peggy Robbins, Brenda Taylor, Charlene Daniel, Faye Harwell, and Mary Hanson. Assistant leader Linda Cochran stands behind the group of girls. (Courtesy of Morgan County Archives.)

A nurse cradles a baby in the maternity ward of Morgan Memorial Hospital around 1965. The vision of a county hospital began in 1957 when citizens indicated that they were in favor of a facility being constructed under the Hill-Burton Act. This program helped provide funding so that small towns could have their own facilities. With funds also raised in the community by selling bonds, the 26-bed facility opened in 1960. (Courtesy of Morgan County Archives.)

Pictured here are Paul and Lula Hurst Atkinson. Lula was known to have mysterious powers that gave her the ability to render objects immobile by simply touching them. In the early 1880s, she toured the country exhibiting these powers, with Paul Atkinson as her manager. In 1885, she retired, and Paul and Lula married and settled in Madison. Paul and his brothers operated Madison Variety Works for a number of years. (Courtesy of Morgan County Heritage website.)

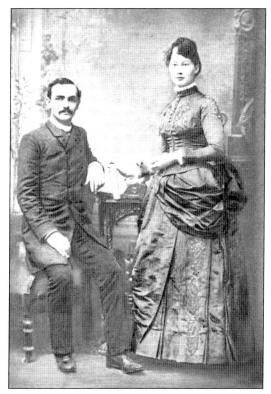

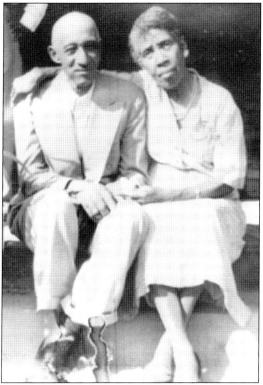

Cleveland and Annie Moore pose in this undated photograph. Cleveland's father, John Wesley Moore, built the house that is now the location of the Morgan County African American Museum. The museum is located next to Calvary Baptist Church in the area of the original settlement that became Madison. (Courtesy of Morgan County Heritage website.)

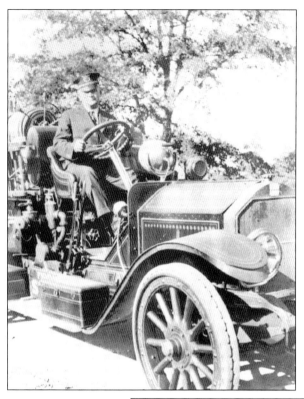

Madison police officer Percy McAdams sits atop the city's 1916 American LaFrance fire engine around 1930. Officer McAdams lost his life serving in the line of duty in Madison. He was attempting to disperse a crowd of men when one of them shot and killed him on August 18, 1931, during a late-night disturbance. McAdams had served as a Madison police officer for three years. Will Mallory, a City of Madison employee, was wounded as well and died about three weeks later. (Courtesy of Morgan County Heritage website.)

Rev. G.L. Allen was the pastor of Calvary Baptist Church in Madison from 1922 to 1938. The site of Calvary Baptist Church on Academy Street was where the Madison Baptist congregation built their first structure, a wood-frame building, in 1834. In the 1870s, the building was moved to Hill Street, where another congregation began their own church, which would eventually become Clark's Chapel Baptist Church. (Courtesy of Morgan County African American Museum.)

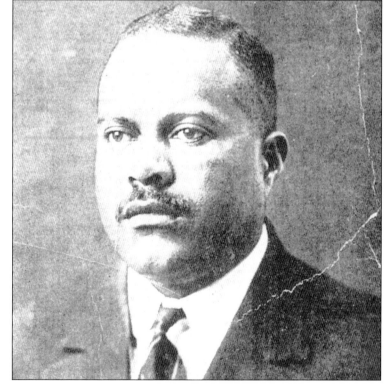

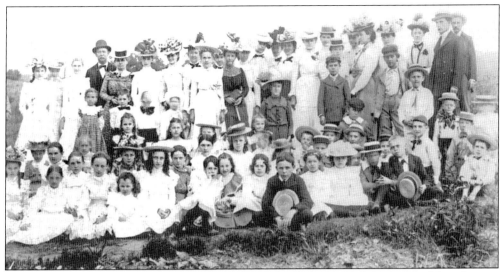

Members of the Madison Baptist Church Sunday school class attend a picnic at Silver Springs in the early 1900s. A Sunday school picnic was a social event that many churches indulged in. Sometimes they joined with another church group to enjoy a day together. (Courtesy of Morgan County Archives.)

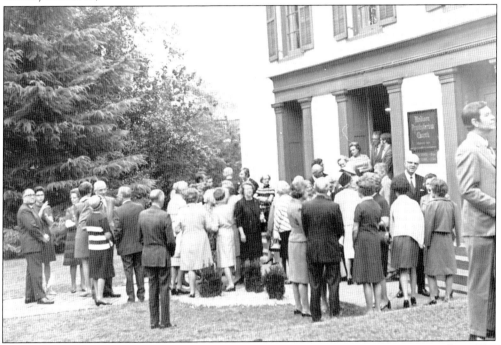

People congregate outside the Madison Presbyterian Church on South Main Street in the 1970s. Sometime in the early 19th century, Presbyterians from Madison and Morgan County decided to begin meeting together. Their earliest services were held in the courthouse and in the Madison Male Academy. The first site purchased was on what is now Porter Street. It was sold in 1842. The present building at 382 South Main Street is Greek Revival and in the style of Doric. It was built by Daniel Killian, a member of the church and a skilled mason. The church was dedicated on the first Sabbath in May 1842. (Courtesy of Morgan County Archives.)

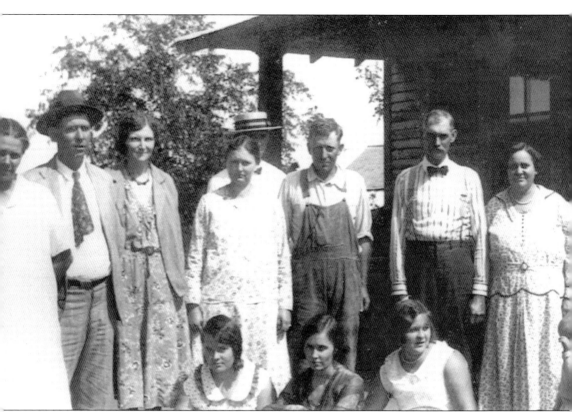

M.P. (Paul) Atkinson and his family are pictured in the 1920s. Affectionately known as the "Brownwood cousins," many members of this branch of the Atkinson family were born and raised in the area and attended Brownwood Baptist Church. After the Civil War, Atharetes Atkinson purchased this land, totaling 600 acres. The family referred to it as "the plantation." (Courtesy of Morgan County Heritage website.)

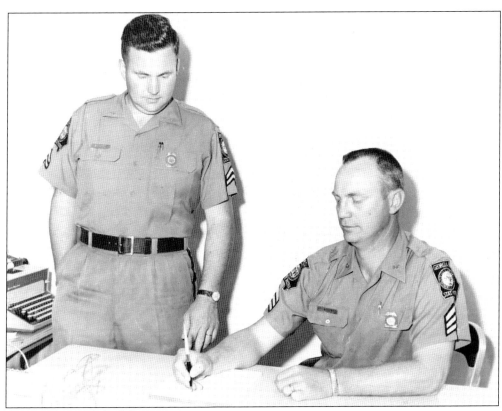

Sgt. Roy Womack (right) assumes duties at the Georgia State Patrol Post in Madison as officer in charge in April 1967. Cpl. Lamar Hawkins (left), second in command, looks on. (Courtesy of Morgan County Archives.)

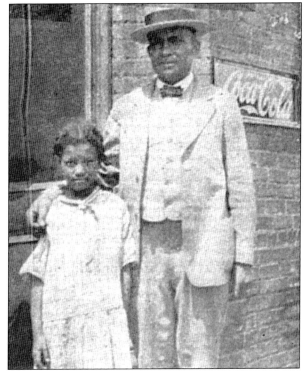

Dr. James F. Smith was a community doctor and leader. He was also very active in church activities and enjoyed music and singing. He and his wife, Eva, ran Star Drugstore in the early 1900s. The pharmacy was very different from those of today. Many medications were made up and mixed on the premises, and the pharmacist was well versed in various academic subjects, such as math, biology, and chemistry as well as homeopathic and herbal remedies. (Courtesy of Morgan County African American Museum.)

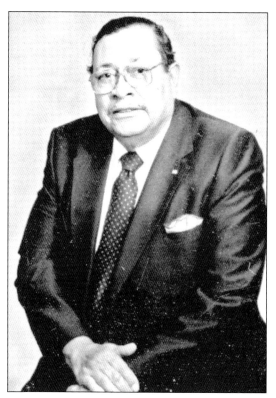

Martin Bass Jr. (1919–1997), shown at left, was born in Madison, graduated from Washington High School in Atlanta, and served in the US Army during World War II. He holds the distinction of being the first African American to have the position of appraiser-reviewer in the United States. From 1958 to 1979, he served as the first honorary consul for the Republic of Liberia, West Africa, for the state of Michigan. He was instrumental in the development of the Morgan County African American Museum. (Courtesy of the Morgan County African American Museum.)

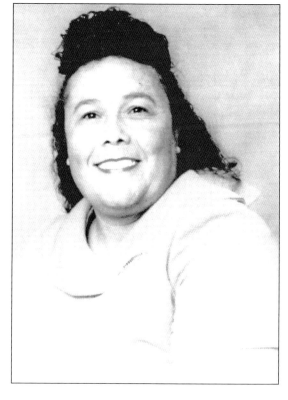

Marie Bass Martin (1921–2006), a community leader and educator, is shown in this photograph. Marie received a bachelor's degree from Savannah State University and a master's degree in education at Atlanta University. She continued her postgraduate studies at Columbia University. She served in the Morgan County School System for 45 years, with 20 of those years as a principal. (Courtesy of the Morgan County African American Museum.)

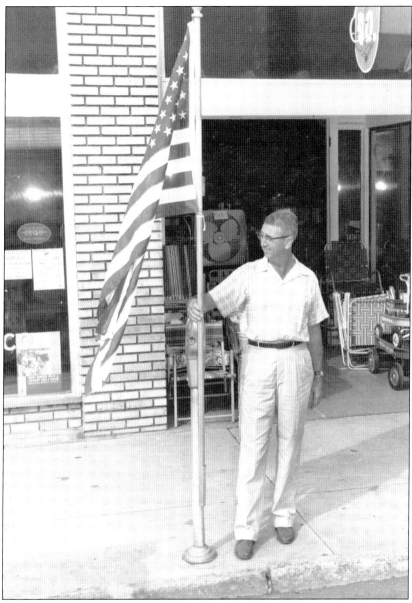

J.D. Harris is pictured in front of his furniture store on West Jefferson Street around 1965. In addition to running Harris Furniture, Harris served the town of Madison in many civic activities, including mayor from 1955 to 1957 and again from 1969 to 1971. In 1943, J.D. bought the languishing Stovall Furniture Company building and the few contents left with his father, John Dillard Harris. The once flourishing business had fallen on hard times due to World War II. To stock their store, the Harrises would cut or buy wood, haul it to manufacturers in Georgia and North Carolina, and bring the furniture back to sell. A sewing plant located across the street employed women in Madison who had gone to work to make ends meet during the war. Harris Furniture sold sewing cabinets, which were very popular with these customers. They set up charge accounts with "a dollar down—a dollar a week" payment system. The Harrises sold the business to Mark Mason in 1975. (Courtesy of Morgan County Archives.)

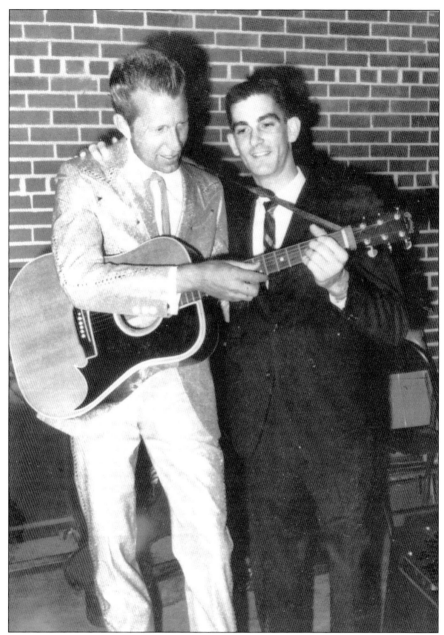

This photograph shows Madison disc jockey John Moody with Porter Wagoner, a famous country music and Grand Ole Opry star in the 1950s. At that time, music stars did not have agents to do their publicity and actually had to take their new recordings to radio stations themselves to add to playlists. When a musician stopped by, he or she was always given an opportunity to sit down in the local radio station and have a live session with the announcer. That was an exciting event to the listeners. There were visits in Madison from Sonny James, Del Reeves, Faron Young, and several other major musicians of the day. Moody was a very talented emcee and was often asked to do the honors at local and out-of-town events. The Madison radio station was once called WMGE but later named WYTH when the Small family owned and operated it for many years. (Courtesy of Connie Shatterly Malone.)

Harold L. Murray was born in Wilkes County, Georgia. He was a graduate of the Chicago Institute of Technology. He became a brick mason and traveled across the United States and Canada. Projects he worked on in Madison include First United Methodist Church, McGeary Hospital, Pearl High School, and the first motel on Eatonton Road. (Courtesy of Morgan County African American Museum.)

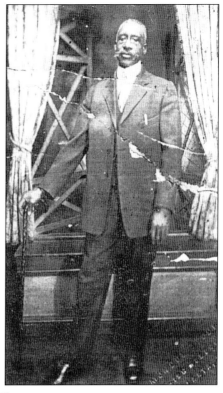

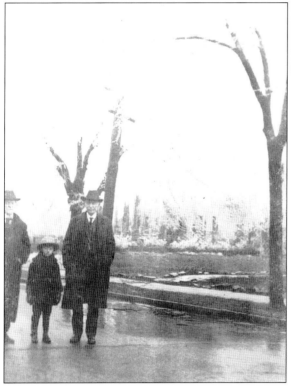

John Grieve McHenry (left), Dan Hicky (center), and an unidentified person survey the damage around Madison following a c. 1924 ice storm. An unidentified Greek Revival–style home in the background is obscured by the trees, which are heavily laden with ice. Tree limbs were beginning to give way, as evidenced by the debris on the ground. (Courtesy of Stratton Hicky.)

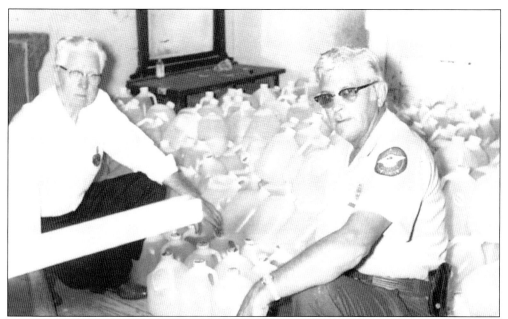

Pictured are J.B. Blackwell (left) and Mike Knight (right) with confiscated moonshine in the 1970s. J.B. Blackwell was the sheriff of Morgan County, and Mike Knight was a deputy. It appears that they discovered perhaps hundreds of gallon jugs of illegal liquor during their raid. The setting is that of an old home, as evidenced by the dresser and fireplace in the background. (Courtesy of Morgan County Heritage website.)

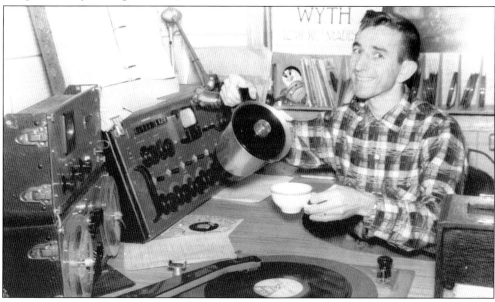

Here is a photograph of John Moody, announcer and disc jockey, playing music at WYTH in the days of live radio. At that time, in the 1960s, it was okay to have coffee and food and even to smoke at the control board—not the case in today's market. This may have been the popular program that John did in the mornings called *Coffee Break*. The program was a mix of current pop songs and big band. He was well known and a favorite of listeners for many years. (Courtesy of Connie Shatterly Malone.)

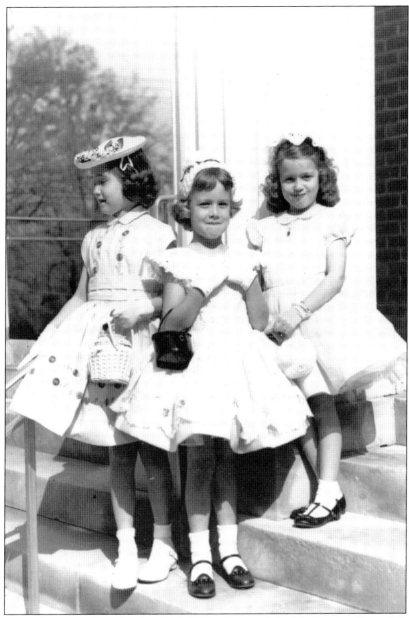

These pretty girls appeared in the April 14, 1960, edition of the *Madisonian*. From left to right, Anna Shouse, Dianne Fitzpatrick, and Teresa Wallace eagerly anticipated the annual Spring Festival, which was held at the Madison High School Auditorium that night. Many people in Madison and in the surrounding countryside bought their new Easter dresses, suits, hats, and shoes at Mack's Department Store or at Gallant-Belk. Mack's was located on West Jefferson Street. It opened on August 31, 1935. In 1958, a fire started in the adjacent building, destroying the store. Mack's was rebuilt one store closer to Main Street. Gallant-Belk was located on South Main Street. It opened on May 28, 1948, at 9:00 a.m. Over 100 excited customers rushed in to see the new store. G.M. Carter, assistant manager of the Gallant-Belk store in Athens, was named manager of the Madison store. Carter retired in 1963, and subsequent managers were Ricky Carter and Larry McCurley (Courtesy of Morgan County Archives.)

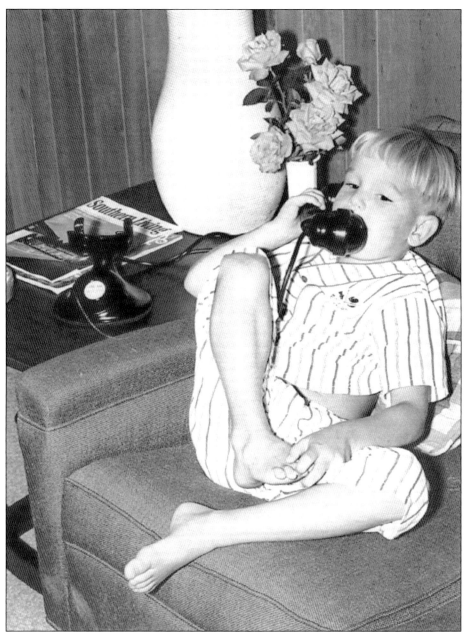

William Dan Pennington, age five, son of state senator Brooks Pennington Jr. and Jacquelyn Christian Pennington, made the last manual telephone call in Madison to his grandmother Lucile Braswell Pennington at 2:00 a.m. on July 16, 1967. Madison was the last Southern Bell exchange in Georgia to convert to dial service from manual operator-assisted service. The Bell system began converting its manual service to dial service in 1920. Some operators who lost their jobs due to the dial service conversion became long-distance operators in other Southern Bell facilities. Atlanta's first dial service came in 1923, and its last conversion to dial service was on the Hemlock exchange in June 1951. Many rural areas in Georgia were slower to convert to dial service than Atlanta. Even when they did, telephone customers in some rural communities were still on party-line systems until the mid-1970s. (Courtesy of Morgan County Heritage website.)

From left to right, Joe, Margaret, and Fannie Love are pictured in this family portrait from the early 1900s. Joe was a tailor who also operated a dry cleaning store. Fannie taught first grade until the late 1950s. Advertisements in the *Madisonian* indicate that there was a dry cleaning business operated by J.K. Love (assumed to be Joe) in the 1960s at 104 West Washington Street. (Courtesy of Morgan County African American Museum.)

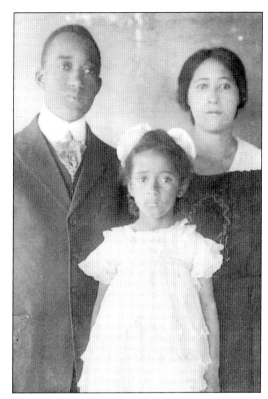

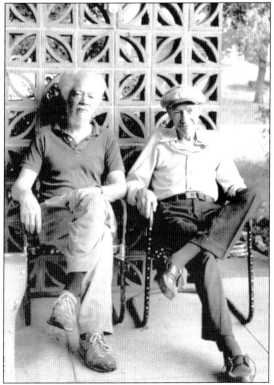

Benny Andrews (left) is pictured with his father, George Andrews. Both are well-known artists from the Madison area. George was known as "the Dot Man" for his prolific use of dots in his works. Benny was the first African American director of the Visual Arts Program of the National Endowment of the Arts, received the Abby Award for lifetime achievement in the arts, and founded the Benny Andrews Foundation for the Benefit of the Arts. (Courtesy of the Morgan County African American Museum.)

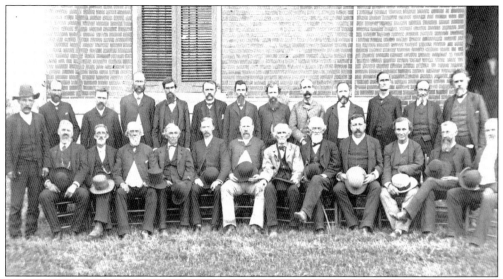

Members of a grand jury in the early 1900s pose next to the Morgan County Courthouse. Atharetes Atkinson is seated fourth from the left. The other men are unidentified. Grand juries have always provided a variety of services to their communities over the years. Georgia grand juries, in addition to reviewing criminal cases, are also required to address inspections and investigations, elections and voting, appointments and nominations, and other miscellaneous duties. (Courtesy of Morgan County Archives.)

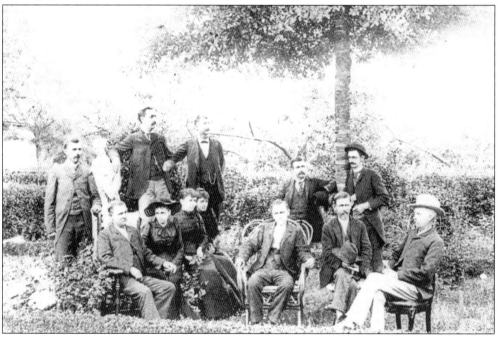

Here is an undated photograph of the Paul and Lula Hurst Atkinson family. They are probably posing at Paul and Lula's home on South Main Street in Madison. Paul was the son of Madison pioneer Atharetes Atkinson. He managed the career of his future wife, Lula Hurst, who was said to have strange powers. When she grew weary of show business, they married and retired to Madison. (Courtesy of Morgan County Heritage website.)

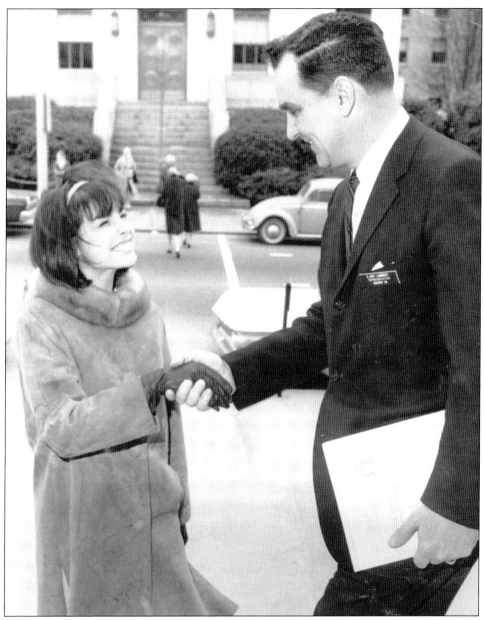

In February 1966, Sen. Roy Lambert (right) of Madison greets Collette Duicete, Miss Teenage America and youth safety spokesman for Lincoln-Mercury Division, at the state capital. She addressed the Georgia legislature, congratulating lawmakers for advancing traffic safety and thanking them for authorizing driver's education programs in Georgia schools. Today, high schools everywhere offer driver's education to students. The class has been offered for many years at Morgan County High School. Concern for the safety of teenagers while driving has led to the passage of a number of laws in Georgia in recent years. These laws include mandatory driver's education, a graduated licensing system, and restrictions on driving before being fully licensed. The most recent law was passed by the Georgia General Assembly in 2010 was Caleb's Law, which prohibits the use of texting devices while driving. The law was named in memory of Caleb Sorohan, an 18-year-old who died in an accident in Morgan County while texting. (Courtesy of Morgan County Archives.)

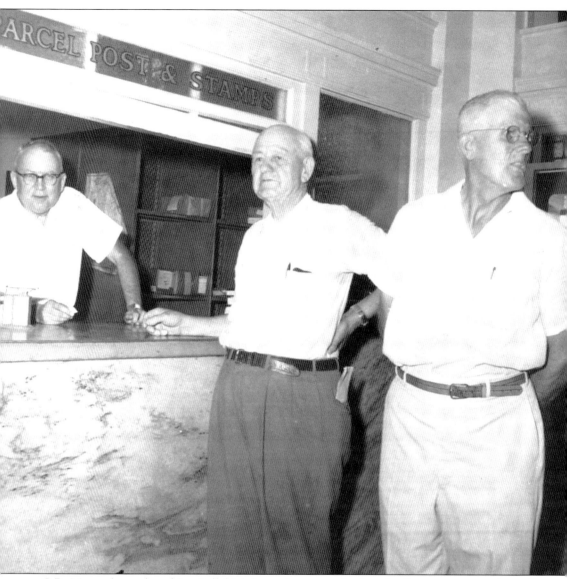

C.R. Mason (center) and Joe Bell (right) are shown purchasing the first commemorative soil conservation stamp sold in Madison from postmaster W.W. Baldwin (left) in September 1959. Bell and Mason were both directors of the Piedmont Soil Conservation Area. The US Post Office is still in use today, located on the square in Madison. Morgan County is in the Piedmont Soil and Water Conservation District, giving agricultural landowners access to educational programs in land management. The 4¢ stamp, titled "The Good Earth," featured a sweeping view of a farm with a city in the distance. It was first released in Rapid City, South Dakota, on August 26, 1959. The US Post Office issued a total of 120,835,000 of this stamp, the first in a series. A water conservation stamp was issued in 1960, and a range stamp was issued in 1961. (Courtesy of Morgan County Archives.)

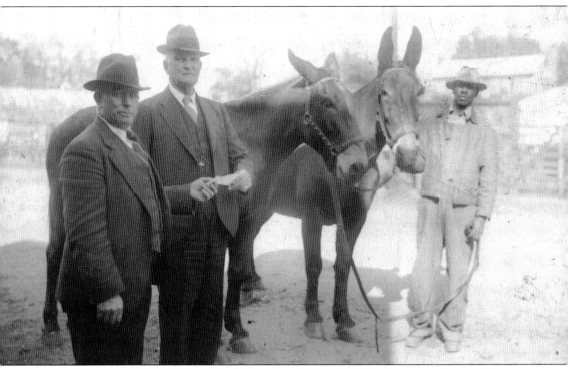

From left to right, Walker Sydney Reid, Pete Bearden, and Buddy Jones are shown with two mules in the early 1930s. Here, Bearden hands a check to Reid for the mules, which were sold at Reid's stables in Madison. This photograph and another one were taken to celebrate the sale of the mules by Reid to Bearden. Bearden was born in Watkinsville in 1863 and died in Atlanta in 1938. During his early years, he played baseball and was a catcher for an Orlando, Florida, team in 1886. The team won the pennant, which is on display in Heritage Hall. He was president of the Bank of Madison from 1927 to 1938. He was an active member of Madison First United Methodist Church and was instrumental in getting the current Methodist church building erected on Main Street in 1914. (Courtesy of Stratton Hicky.)

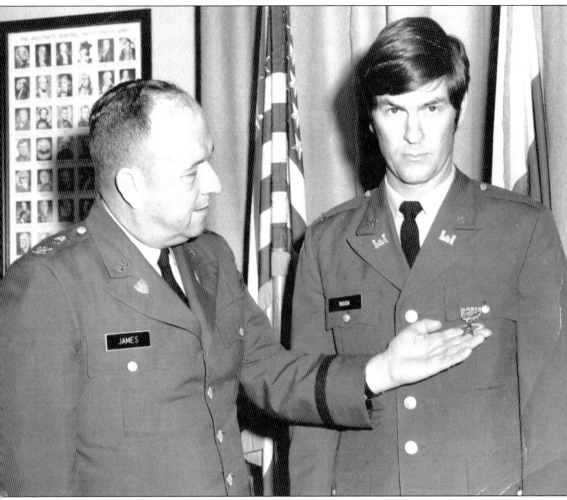

First Lt. Carl F. Riden Jr. is awarded the Bronze Star Medal with "V" device at Third US Army Headquarters by Col. W.H. James prior to his discharge from the US Army in January 1972. The medal was presented to Riden for his service in Vietnam as platoon leader of the equipment platoon of Company A, 815th Engineer Battalion (Construction). Lieutenant Riden served in the office of the adjutant general at Third US Army Headquarters. The "V" device represents valor. While the medal itself is awarded for merit, the addition of the "V" device is based on acts of heroism. The Bronze Star Medal was established by Executive Order in 1944. It is the fourth highest combat award given by the US armed forces. Carl is the son of Carl Franklin Riden Sr. and Sara Malcom Riden of Morgan County. (Courtesy of Morgan County Archives.)

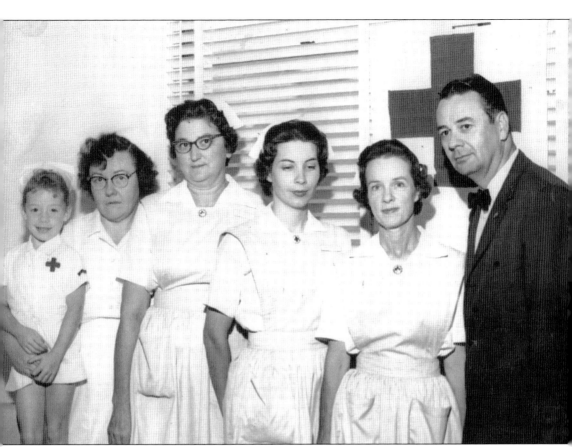

Nurses who were on the staff of Morgan Memorial Hospital when it opened in 1960 are pictured here. From left to right are Page Walker, unidentified, Claudine Conner Craig, Ona Malcom Nunn, Katherine Everett, and a hospital administrator. Morgan Memorial also had an active nurse's aide training program. Ceremonies to pin those who completed the program were held several times a year. The opening of the hospital was eagerly anticipated and was a major event for the community. The much smaller McGeary Hospital downtown had closed in the mid-1950s, leaving the area without a convenient emergency treatment facility for several years. When the hospital opened, it was lauded as one of the most advanced rural facilities of its kind in the country. (Courtesy of Morgan County Heritage website.)

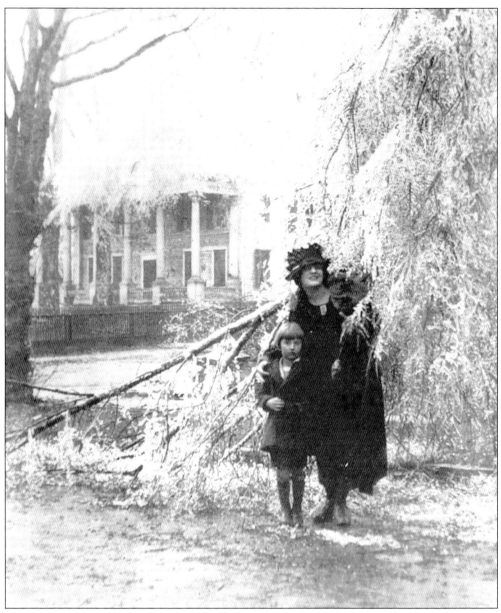

Dan Hicky (left) and Hallie McHenry Shinholser (right) are seen in front of the Porter-Fitzpatrick home following an ice storm around 1920. By this time, trees had already begun to break with the weight of the ice. The two are standing amongst the limbs of a large branch that has fallen into South Main Street. Hallie was Dan's aunt and the sister of Louise McHenry Hicky. The Hicky family lived on Old Post Road (known then as South Second Street) in the Stokes-McHenry House. Ice storms brought all travel to a halt and threatened to knock down power poles. Not much has changed today—towns are still paralyzed by snow and ice in the South. At the time this photograph was taken, most rural residents in Morgan County outside the town of Madison probably did not have electricity, and many did not have cars. Even though they were isolated, ironically, they were probably the ones least impacted negatively by this type of weather. (Courtesy of Stratton Hicky.)

Moses Bass was the first freed slave to purchase land in Morgan County. Since he could neither read nor write, he signed the deed for the purchase with an X. He encouraged his family to get an education, as he never had the opportunity to do so himself. Bass was born in 1847 and died in 1918. He was the great-grandfather of Martin Bass Jr. and Marie Bass Martin. (Courtesy of Morgan County African American Museum.)

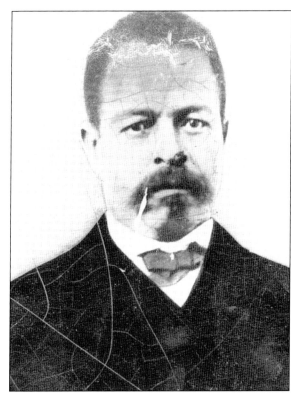

Luther J. Yarbrough is shown in April 1958 at the linotype machine at the *Madisonian*. Yarbrough worked on linotype machines at various newspapers for over 52 years. He came to the *Madisonian* in May 1937. He passed away on October 25, 1967. (Courtesy of Morgan County Archives.)

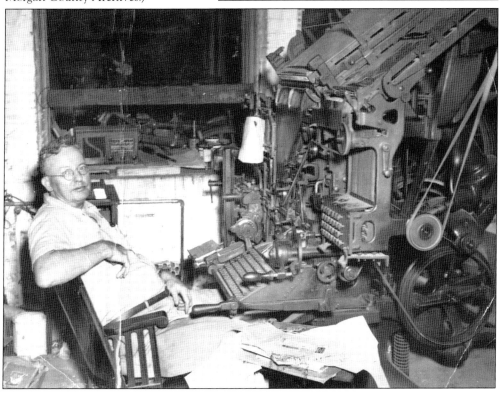

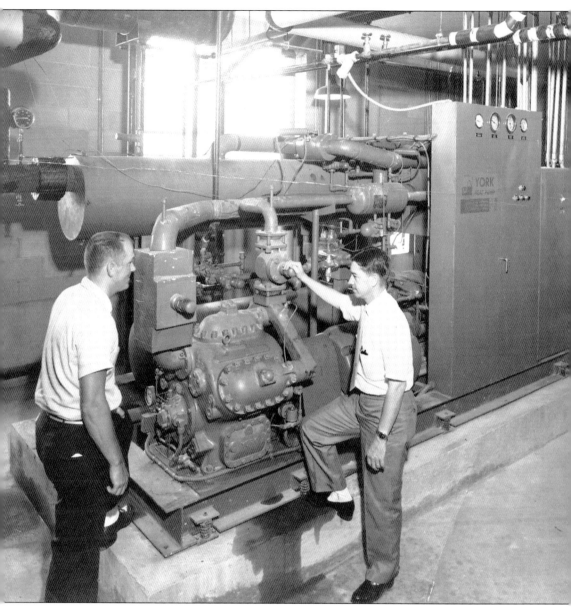

Elbert Shaw Jr. (above, left), administrator at Morgan Memorial Hospital, examines the heating and cooling system, controlled by a heat pump, at the hospital, along with the system's designer in July 1959. The brand-new hospital was preparing to open the following January. At the time, the heating and cooling system was called one of the best in the country. Shaw had been the administrator for six months when the hospital opened. Before that, a hospital board managed the planning of the facility. The new hospital also featured modern diagnostic and communication equipment. The town was proud of its new facility, which was able to pump oxygen into patients' rooms. The new building also included a stainless steel kitchen with a heated food service. The building was constructed at a cost of $500,000. Cost of the new equipment was $60,000. Patient-room equipment, office equipment, lounge and office furniture, and other items were funded through memorial gifts. More than 1,000 people attended the hospital's open house. (Courtesy of Morgan County Archives.)

Two

SCENES ABOUT TOWN

To visitors, the town of Madison may seem like an idyllic, quiet village. However, the shady, tree-lined streets, historic homes, and quaint downtown storefronts belie a more dynamic and vibrant city. Over the years a variety of businesses and industries have thrived in the small town. Agriculture has played a significant role in the development of Madison. The town has also been a center of educational, religious, and civic activities for many years. The scenes in this chapter tell the story of Madison through its physical sites over the years. Some of these buildings no longer stand. Others have been altered over time and appear very different.

There are many layers of history in the buildings and the grounds of this town, and this chapter only begins to explore those layers. The people of Madison are shown in many of these photographs, making them more than just pictures of buildings. They are pictures of life in Madison.

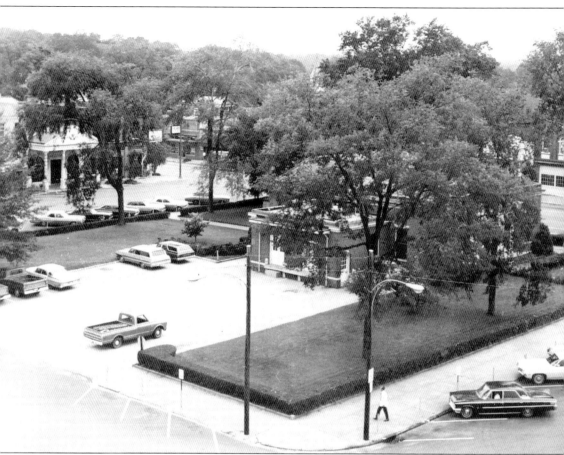

The town square is seen from the top of the Morgan County Courthouse in the early 1970s. The view is toward the northwest. Downtown businesses can be seen in the distance beyond the US Post Office. The Sears sign hangs above Main Street. The partially obscured Ye Old Colonial Restaurant sign juts out at the corner of Main and East Washington Streets. Next door is the old Bank of Madison building, which was purchased by Joe Cunningham and added to Ye Old Colonial. The bank vault, papered with Reconstruction money, still resides in the former bank area to the delight of restaurant customers. Baldwin's Pharmacy and Madison Drugs on Main Street are hidden by the trees towering over the post office. It appears that the parking meters, which were such a point of contention with Madison drivers, have been removed and only the poles still stand. (Courtesy of Morgan County Heritage website.)

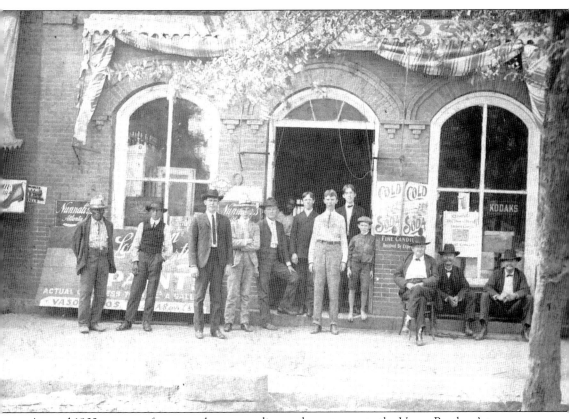

Around 1902, a group of men are shown standing at the entrance to the Vason Brothers' store on Main Street in downtown Madison. Walker Sydney Reid (1885–1975), age 17 at the time, stands on the step wearing a suit with a white tie. Reid, the son of J.S. Reid Jr., owned a livery stable in Madison. The other men are unidentified. Over the years, this building has housed a variety of retail merchandise and grocery stores and other similar types of businesses. The building recently became the new home of Antique Sweets, a family-owned and -operated candy store started by Patty and Patrick Alligood in 2004. This is one of the brick buildings that dominate several streets in the town. The brick buildings were constructed after the fire of 1869 destroyed most of the wood-frame businesses downtown. (Courtesy of Stratton Hicky.)

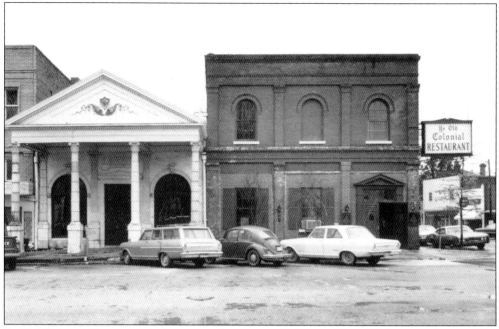

Ye Old Colonial Restaurant is located at the corner of Main and East Washington Streets. The restaurant was originally called The Grille. In January 1966, a fire destroyed The Grille and damaged the cellar and the attic. Roy Lambert's and Raymond Jones's offices were next door in the old bank building. Lambert climbed on the roof with the firefighters and workers to help control the damage. Owner Joe Cunningham reopened the restaurant, changing the name. It is believed that the cellar area, known as the "Rebel Cellar" in the 1960s, dates to the late 18th century, prior to the existence of the town. (Courtesy of Morgan County Archives.)

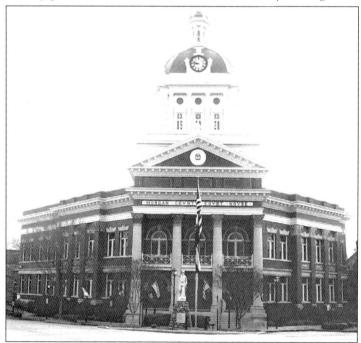

The current Morgan County Courthouse stands at the corner of Hancock and East Jefferson Streets. The building was finished in 1907. Until that time, the courthouse stood on the square. The structure that served as the courthouse prior to this one was used as office space and a theater after the county offices moved into this building. The old structure burned around 1916. (Photograph by Marcia Brooks.)

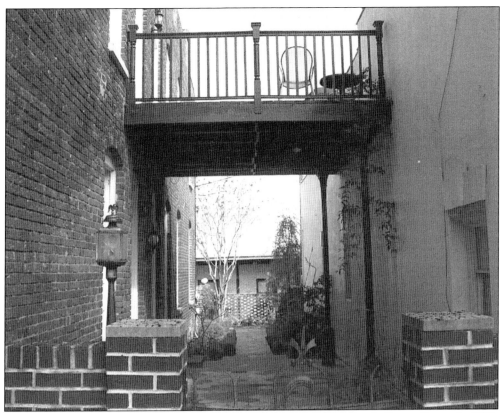

A narrow gap between buildings allows for a secluded courtyard on East Jefferson Street. In 1970, the old Madisonian building to the right was remodeled for office space by Dr. M. Kinstein. The offices and printing facilities of the *Madisonian* moved to the building at left, and this area was designed as a garden based on plans by landscape architect June Harrell. (Photograph by Marcia Brooks.)

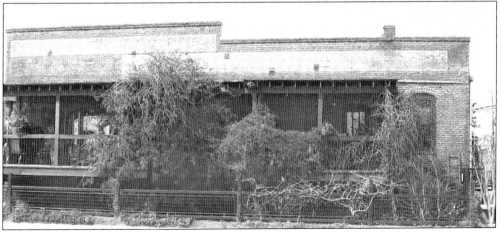

The Ice House was located on West Jefferson Street near the railroad tracks. This business provided blocks of ice to customers for use in preserving food before homes had refrigerators. The building stood empty for many years until it was converted into a combination restaurant and loft condominiums in the 2000s. (Courtesy of Marcia Brooks.)

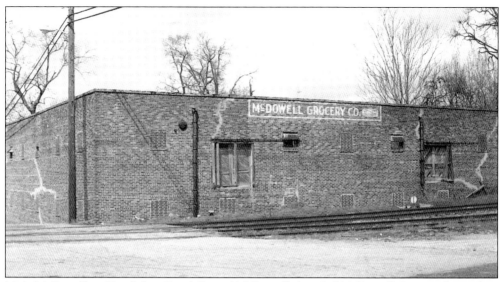

M.A. McDowell and his father, Frank Daniel McDowell, founded McDowell Grocery, located on West Jefferson Street near the railroad, about 1916. Originally, this was a small wooden building, purchased from Rosa Parker. The building was subsequently bricked and enlarged. Little Miss cornmeal, one of the most popular brands in the area, was milled here for many years. (Photograph by Marcia Brooks.)

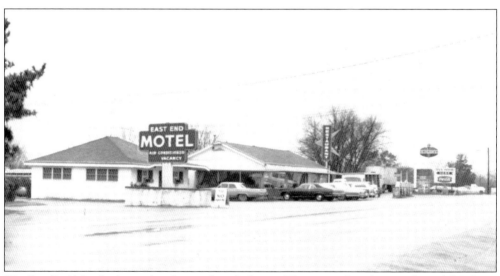

The East End Motel is located at the north end of town. Those traveling from or through Madison to Athens have passed this location on the right since the early 1960s. The motel included a restaurant that locals as well as travelers enjoyed. When this photograph was taken in 1967, an American Oil Company (Amoco) service station stood next door. A used car lot now occupies the space approximately where the gas station was. (Courtesy of Morgan County Archives.)

A fire on Main Street engulfs the top floor of the Variety Store in 1939, also threatening other businesses. This photograph was taken from the corner of Main and East Washington Streets. No other stores sustained major damage, but the top floor was never rebuilt. The store later became Armour's Five & Ten. (Courtesy of Morgan County Heritage website.)

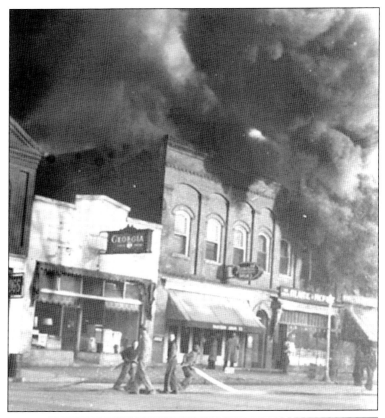

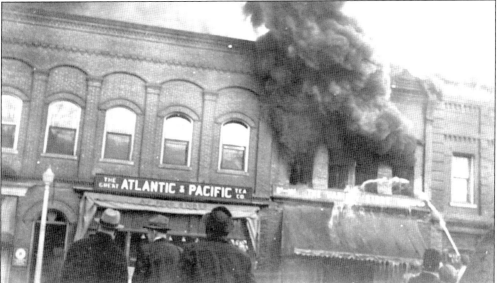

In this closer view of the fire on Main Street in 1939, firefighters try to tackle the fire as bystanders look on. This photograph was taken from the front lawn of the US Post Office on the square. It is evident that the top floor of the building was fully engulfed. The adjacent buildings still bear faint marks from where the second floor was attached to them. (Courtesy of Morgan County Heritage website.)

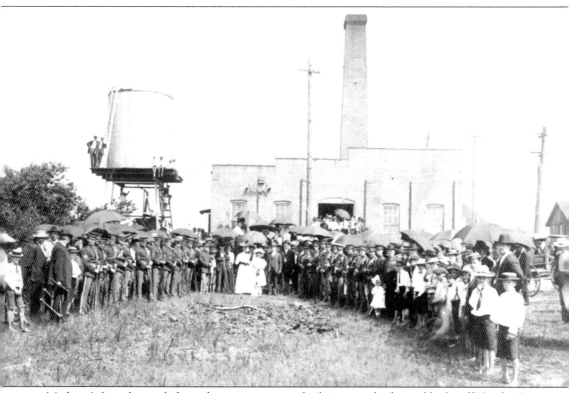

Madison's first electric light and pumping station facilities were built two blocks off North Main Street at the corner of North Second and Burney Streets. Pictured are residents celebrating the ground breaking of the first waterworks facilities in 1908, with the electric plant, built in 1892, in the background. The waterworks facilities included a 118,000-gallon tank (pictured at left) and a standpipe with 102,000-gallon capacity. Water was distributed throughout the town in six-inch and eight-inch pipes under the streets. Modern buildings in the same vicinity have now replaced the old waterworks facilities. The origins of Madison were based on availability of water. The area of Round Bowl Springs, near Calvary Baptist Church on Academy Street, was a gathering spot for Native Americans. In time, a settlement was established at this location, which eventually became Madison. (Courtesy of Morgan County Heritage website.)

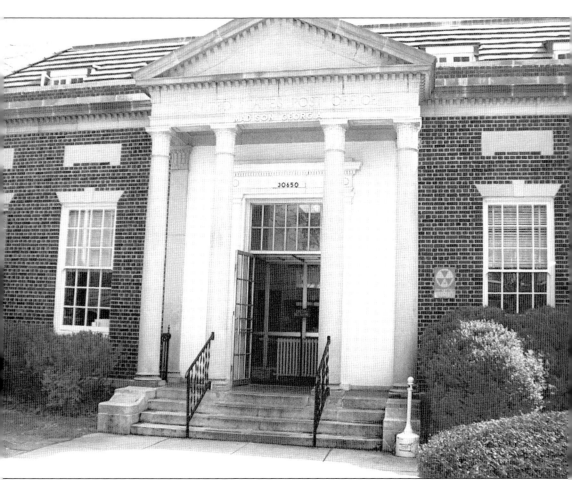

The Madison Post Office is located on the square, the former site of the Morgan County Courthouse. After the second courthouse burned in 1916, the property was sold to the federal government on the condition that it would be used for the good of the townspeople. When it was decided that the post office would be built here in the 1930s, some citizens were opposed to such use of the property and tried to obtain an injunction to stop the construction. In spite of their efforts, the building was constructed. (Photograph by Marcia Brooks.)

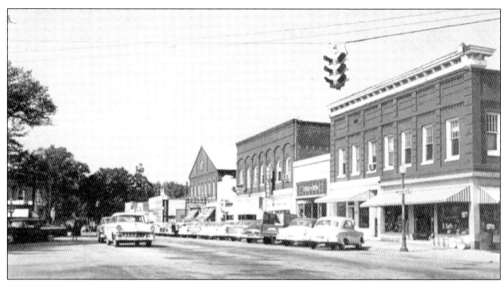

Downtown Madison is shown here in the early 1960s. The view is looking south on Main Street. Straight ahead on the corner of Main and East Washington Streets is The Grille, which later became Ye Old Colonial Restaurant. The US Post Office is out of the frame to the left. Businesses visible in the block on the right side of the picture included Baldwin's Pharmacy, Madison Drugs, and Butler's Furniture Co. (Courtesy of Morgan County Heritage website.)

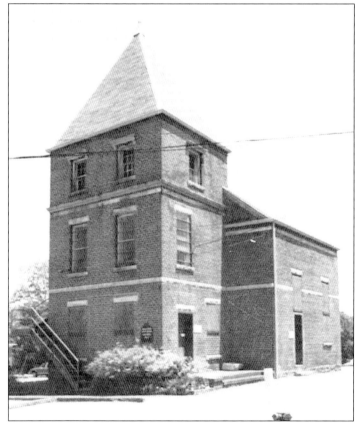

This building is the location of the old Madison jailhouse, built in 1892. Cell doors and other features of late-19th-to-early-20th-century jails are still present in this building. At least one hanging is said to have occurred in the building. It is currently the home of the Morgan County Archives. Marshall "Woody" Williams, former county historian and archivist, rescued many historical documents and photographs from destruction and has modified a portion of the jail to house the records. (Courtesy of Morgan County Heritage website.)

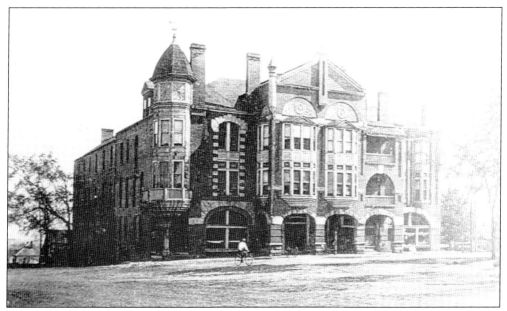

The New Morgan Hotel stood on Hancock Street across from the site of the current courthouse. This hotel operated during the late 19th and early 20th centuries. During its first year of operation, it was run by Oliver Hardy, the father of Norvell Hardy, who had adopted his father's name by the time he became famous. The actor Oliver Hardy lived in Madison as a boy and attended first grade at the Madison Graded School (now Madison-Morgan Cultural Center). (Courtesy of Morgan County Heritage website.)

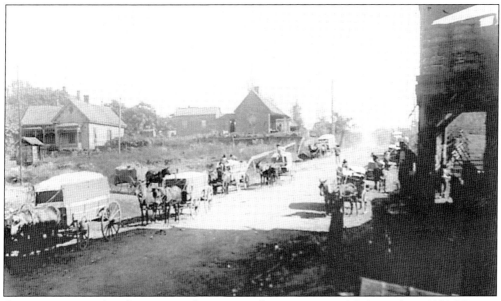

Cotton wagons are lined up waiting their turn at the cotton gin in Madison about 1908. The gin was located near the railroad trestle on West Washington Street. The view is from just beyond the trestle looking back toward the center of town. The homes on the left are gone, and Madison's Town Park now stands in their place. (Courtesy of Morgan County Heritage website.)

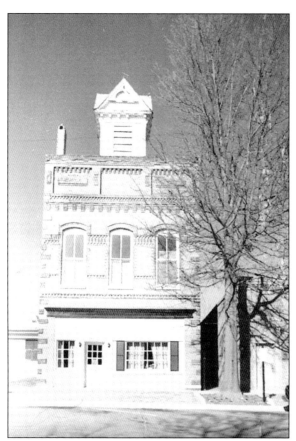

The Madison Chamber of Commerce building on East Jefferson Street originally served as Madison City Hall. It was built in 1887. It included a firehouse and jail. After the third (current) courthouse was constructed, the mayor and city clerk's offices were moved to the vacated courthouse building on the square in 1909. Some of the city records were lost when fire destroyed the old courthouse building in 1916. (Courtesy of Morgan County Heritage website.)

In this photograph from about 1970, taken from the courthouse tower, the First National Bank is on the left and across Hancock Street at the corner of Jefferson Street is Simmons Funeral Home. The First National Bank was originally opened on East Jefferson Street in 1904. In the mid-1960s, it relocated to this site. It presently operates as a Suntrust bank branch. (Courtesy of Morgan County Heritage website.)

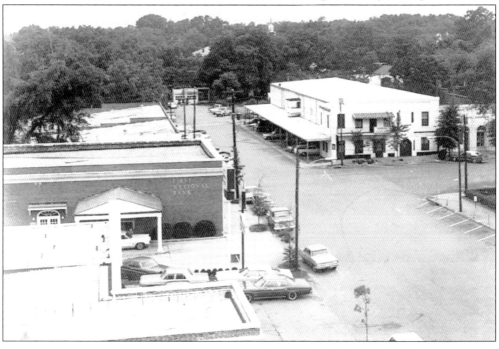

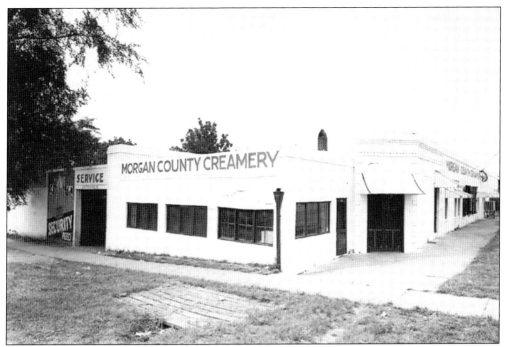

Dairy farmers in Morgan County took their fresh milk to the Morgan County Creamery to have the cream separated. The milk was then hauled to milk distributors in Atlanta by truck and from there shipped to Tennessee. The business was opened at the south end of Hancock Street in 1949. In 1955, the business began making cheese for Kraft Foods. A second story has been added, and the building currently houses county government offices. (Courtesy of Morgan County Heritage website.)

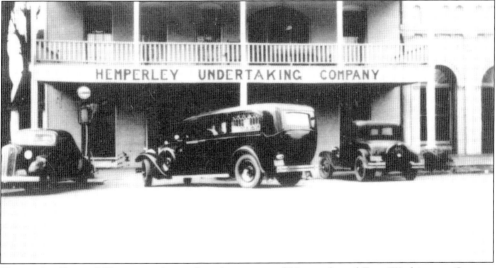

Hemperley Funeral Home was located at the corner of Hancock and East Washington Streets. This building was used as a funeral home for many years and was run by at least three different undertakers over time. Prior to Hemperley, L.M. Thompson Funeral Home was located here. After Hemperley, Simmons Funeral Home operated here until the late 2000s. (Courtesy of Morgan County Heritage website.)

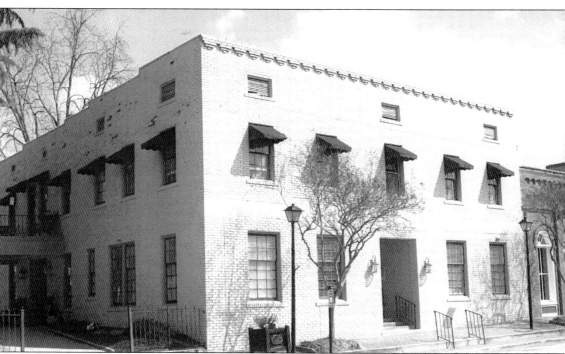

This building on West Jefferson Street was the location of the second hospital in Madison, known as McGeary Hospital. The first hospital opened in 1931 on Main Street in the upstairs portion of the Vason Building (former location of Madison Drugs) by Dr. William Clyde McGeary Sr. The small facility had equipment that was considered modern for its day. Nurses were staffed there, and medical and surgical services were offered. In 1935, an X-ray machine was added. In 1938, Dr. McGeary purchased the Payne Building on West Jefferson Street with plans to enlarge the hospital. At the time, the building housed a restaurant and bicycle shop. In February 1939, a fire destroyed the top floor of the Trammel Building next to the Vason Building, also partially destroying the hospital facilities upstairs. Remodeling had already begun on the Payne Building, and in April 1939, the new structure opened as McGeary Hospital. It remained in use until May 1954 and was later used as doctors' offices and a nursing home. It is now known as Moore Retirement Center. (Courtesy of Marcia Brooks.)

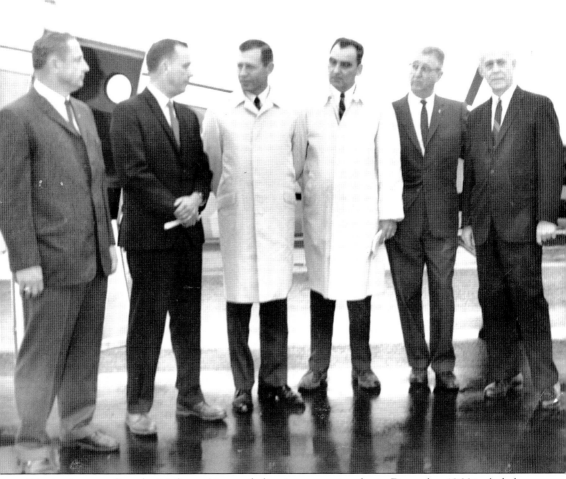

Dignitaries attending the Madison Airport dedication on a rainy day in December 1966 included, from left to right, Dick Norton, Brooks Pennington, Georgia governor Carl Sanders, Roy Lambert, J.D. Harris, and W.M. McClure. Governor Sanders was instrumental in helping Morgan County obtain funding to build the airport. The airport was built on land on the north side of town, off US Highway 441. During his term of office, Sanders made it possible for many rural Georgia communities to get airports. Sanders believed that increasing the number of airports would create economic opportunities for small towns. During his campaign for governor, he spent a lot of time flying. His plane was often forced to land on cow pastures or old World War II airfields. Because of these experiences, he made a decision that improvements would be made to the airport situation in Georgia. As an incentive to local governments, he obtained the federal funding to build airports if the local jurisdiction would purchase the land. (Courtesy of Morgan County Archives.)

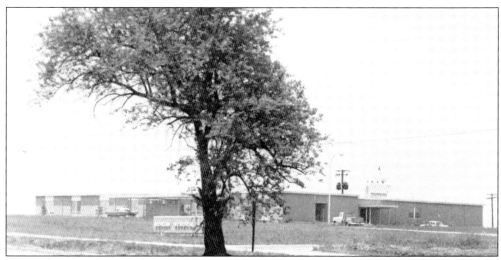

Morgan Memorial Hospital opened a new 26-bed hospital in January 1960. It is located on the Atlanta Highway (US Highway 278) just outside the Madison Historic District in the Canterbury Park area of town. At the time of its opening, it was considered one of the most modern hospitals in the state. A nurse call system, which allowed communication between nurses and patients in their rooms, was considered a special innovative feature at the time. (Courtesy of Morgan County Archives.)

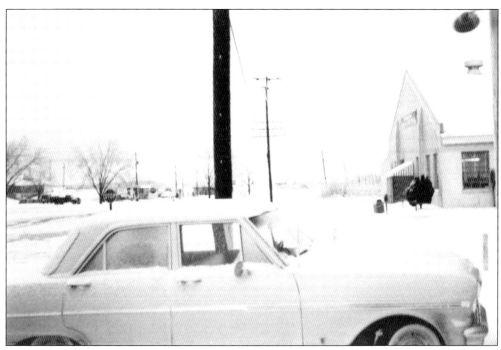

A February 1963 snowstorm makes for a beautiful view across Eatonton Road (US Highway 441) from the parking lot of WYTH. The view faces the general direction of the land on which retail stores would later be built. At the time of this photograph, it was farmland. (Courtesy of Connie Shatterly Malone.)

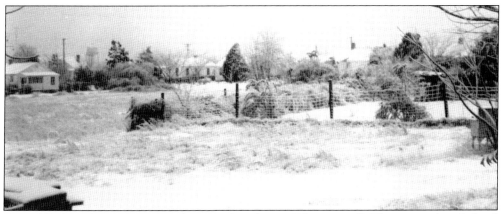

A rare blanket of snow dressed Madison in white lace in February 1963. This view is from behind Madison's radio station WYTH looking toward part of the Beacon Heights subdivision. One of Madison's water towers can be seen in the distance. (Courtesy of Connie Shatterly Malone.)

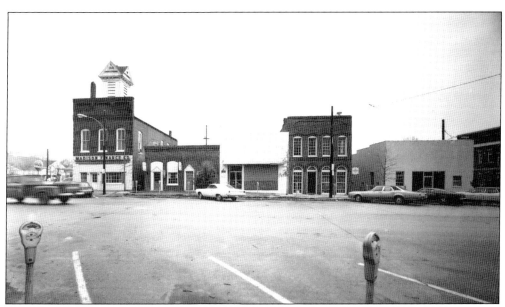

This undated photograph shows East Jefferson Street from the square. The block at this time included a barbershop and beauty salon, Madison Finance Company, an insurance agency, and the *Madisonian* offices. A Union 76 service station stood on the corner of East Jefferson and Main Streets. (Courtesy of Morgan County Archives.)

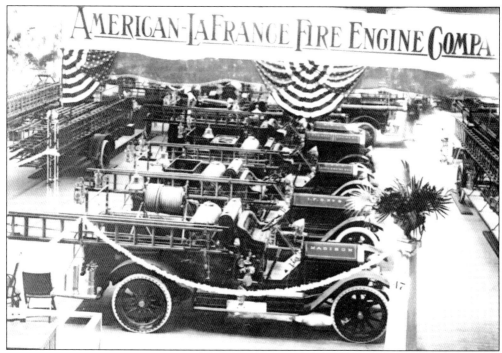

This photograph shows new fire engines made by the American LaFrance Fire Engine Company on display at the Rhode Island Fire Chief's Conference in 1916. Madison's new engine is the first in the line, as evidenced by the name of the city on the hood of the engine. The City of Madison allowed the manufacturer to show the engine at the conference, prior to its delivery to Madison via rail. (Courtesy of Morgan County Heritage website.)

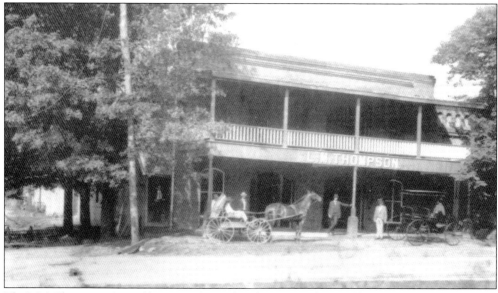

The L.M. Thompson funeral home was located at the corner of East Jefferson and Hancock Streets. This undated photograph was taken before extensive modifications were made to the building. Thompson established the business in 1890 at this location. It was sold in the early 1900s to W.C. Hemperly and then to John Simmons in 1970. (Courtesy of Morgan County Heritage website.)

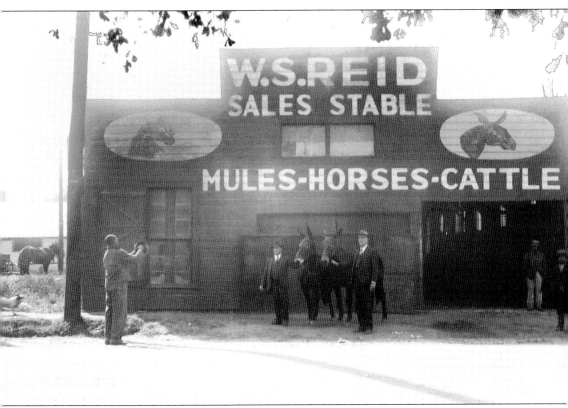

Walker Sydney Reid (1885–1975) stands to the left of two mules, and Pete Bearden stands to the right in the 1930s. The location is W.S. Reid Sales Stable on West Washington Street, near Madison's Town Park. This photograph and another one were taken to celebrate the sale of the mules by Reid to Bearden. (Courtesy of Stratton Hicky.)

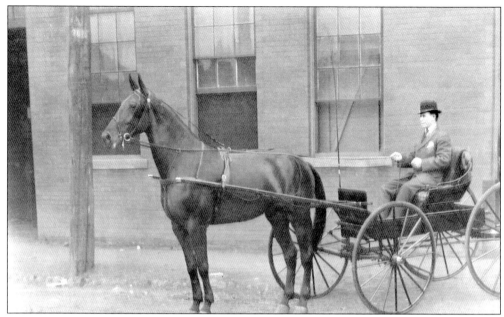

W.S. Reid (1885–1975) is pictured with his new horse and carriage in the 1910s. Reid was the son of James Sydney Reid Jr. (1861–1917) and Mina Reta Walker (1869–1894). He owned and operated the W.S. Reid Sales Stable in Madison. There were several livery stables in the town prior to the widespread use of automobiles. (Courtesy of Stratton Hicky.)

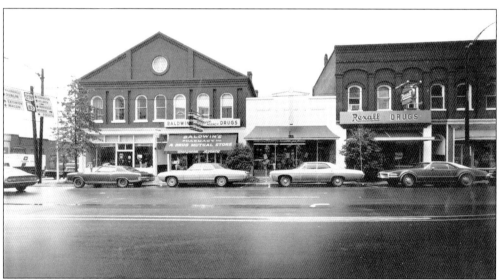

Pictured is Main Street at the corner of West Washington Street about 1970. This part of the block included Baldwin's Pharmacy and Madison Drugs, Baldwin Realty, attorney Eugene Baldwin's office, and at least two other retail businesses. One of the town's controversial parking meters can be seen in this photograph. (Courtesy of Morgan County Archives.)

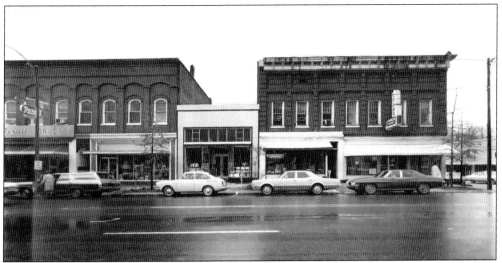

Pictured is Main Street at the corner of West Jefferson Street about 1970. To the right of Madison Drugs are an unidentified retail business, Armour's Five & Ten, a fabric store, Franklin Discount Loans, and offices of attorney A.F. Jenkins, insurance agent C.M. Furlow, and an unidentified dentist. In the background to the right is Mack's Department Store on West Jefferson Street. (Courtesy of Morgan County Archives.)

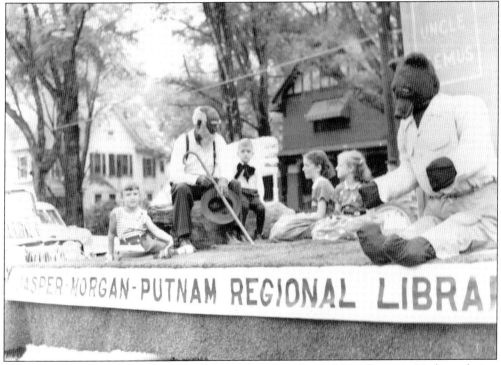

The Jasper-Morgan-Putnam Regional Library float parades up Main Street in Madison during the Morgan County sesquicentennial celebration in 1957. The library system, headquartered in Madison, has always been known as the Uncle Remus Regional Library. Pictured are, from left to right, Martha Brown, Emory Tucker (as Uncle Remus), Tommy Thompson, and Janice and Elaine Wallace. (Courtesy of Morgan County Library.)

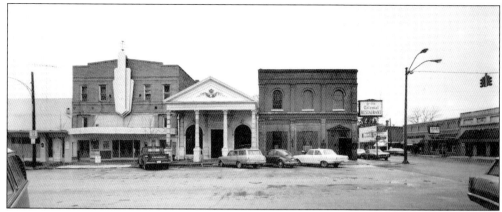

Pictured is East Washington Street around 1970. At this time, the block included the Madison Theatre, which closed in 1973. Ye Old Colonial Restaurant is at the corner of East Washington and Main Streets. At this time, the block also included the law office of Roy Lambert. In the background to the right, businesses can be seen on South Main Street, including the Sears catalog store that was operated by Henry Carson. (Courtesy o f Morgan County Archives.)

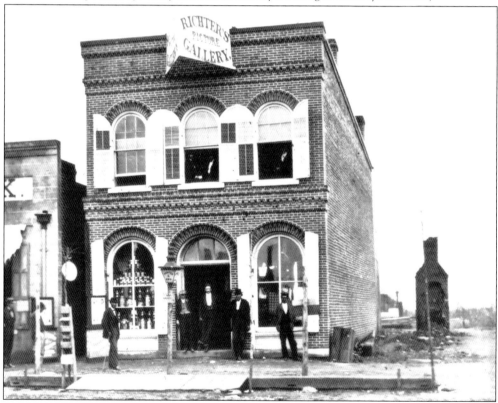

This photograph of Richter's Picture Gallery was taken in 1878, nine years after a devastating fire that destroyed most of the downtown buildings. The chimney of a burned building stands to the right of the business. Prior to the fire, most of Madison's downtown buildings were constructed of wood. As a result of the fire, the town rebuilt most of the structures with brick. This building still stands on South Main Street and currently houses a real estate office. (Courtesy of Morgan County Heritage website.)

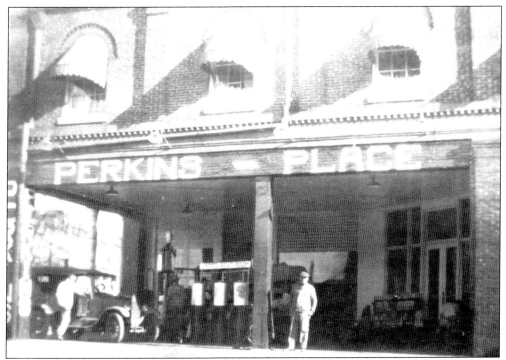

Pictured is Perkins Place gas station in 1926. The building stands at the corner of Main and East Washington Streets in the center of town and presently houses Ye Old Colonial Restaurant. By this time, Main Street was paved and had become a state route. With no bypasses or interstates to divert early travelers, this was an ideal location for a gas station. (Courtesy of Morgan County Heritage website.)

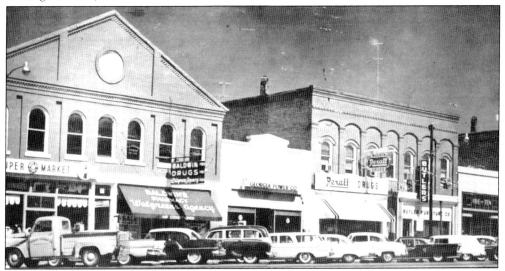

This photograph shows Main Street (also US Highway 441/278) as it appeared in 1956. The location is directly across from where the US Post Office stands today on the site of two earlier courthouses. Included in this photograph are White Dot Supermarket, Baldwin's Pharmacy, Georgia Power Co., Madison Drugs, Butler Furniture Company, and Armour's Five & Ten. (Courtesy of Morgan County Heritage website.)

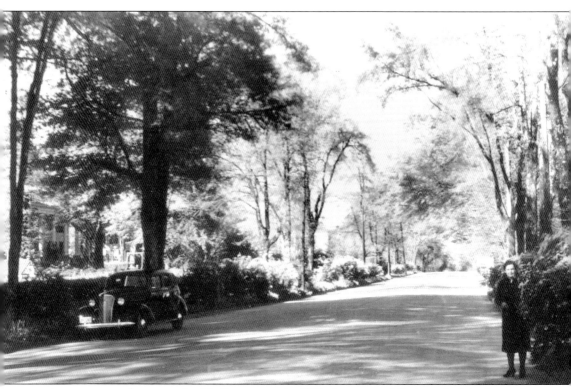

A woman stands on a quiet Madison street in 1937. An automobile is parked in front of an antebellum home that is obscured by trees and engulfed in shade. To the left of the home, a diminutive miniature building with Victorian elements stands waiting, perhaps for a child to come and play. The woman's coat gives one the sense that the picture was taken in late fall or early spring. Other homes along the street peek out, showing only a fraction of their splendor. The leaves of the mature trees allow filtered sunlight to dapple the street. The trees of Madison are an integral element of its charm. They provide an atmosphere that refreshes the senses and calms the mind. Madison has nurtured its trees through the years, allowing them to help define the character of the town. (Courtesy of Morgan County Archives.)

Three

CHURCHES, MONUMENTS, AND TRIBUTES

Throughout its history, the residents of Madison have actively participated in church functions. Over the years, Madison has been home to a variety of religious denominations, including Roman Catholic, Episcopal, Presbyterian, Methodist, Baptist, and Seventh-day Adventist. A church has occupied the site where the town was founded since the town's beginning.

The churches of Madison have a rich and storied history of their own. Legend has it that all three churches currently located on South Main Street played roles in the Civil War. Several African American churches played important roles in town development following the Civil War. Madison's churches have been the site of countless weddings, funerals, baccalaureate services, and other events marking important points in life.

Madison also takes the time to pay tribute to heroes and loved ones. Several monuments have been placed around the town over the years, and its cemeteries contain many beautiful statues and markers of remembrance. The churches, monuments, and cemeteries of Madison provide a grounding force for the town, allowing it to maintain a sense of spirituality and reverence for the past. The people of Madison treasure pleasant memories of the past, but also remember and learn from the tragedies the town has experienced and look with eager anticipation toward the future by preserving these important features of the town.

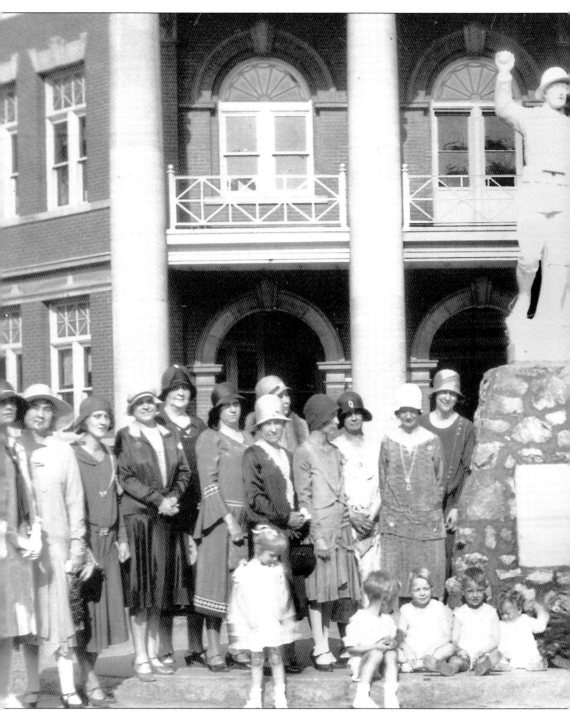

On Sunday, May 4, 1930, residents of Madison gathered in front of the Morgan County Courthouse for the dedication of Morgan County's doughboy statue. The Henry Walton Chapter of the Daughters of the American Revolution erected the monument. The inscription reads, "In memory of the boys from Morgan County, Georgia who fought in the World War April 6, 1917–November 11, 1918." Similar statues were placed in cities throughout the country to commemorate the sacrifices

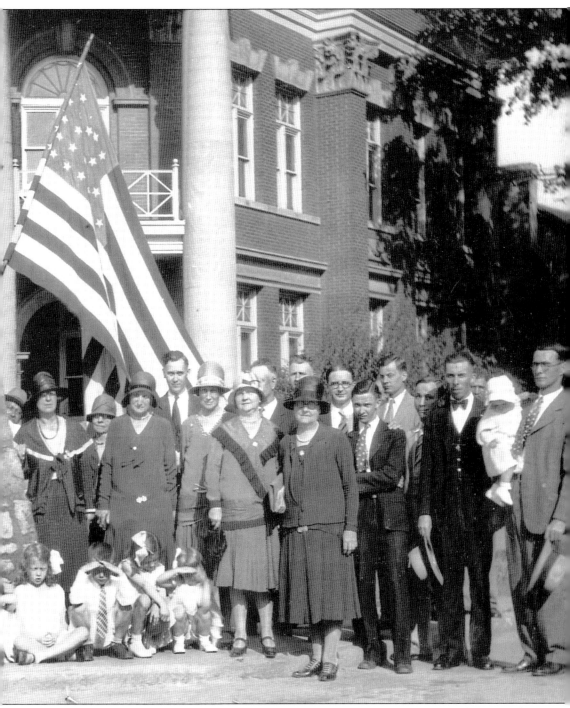

of the soldiers in World War I. Ernest Moore Visquesney designed the work, called the *Spirit of the American Doughboy*. It is the image of an American infantryman making his way through No Man's Land with his rifle in his left hand and a grenade in his right hand. Morgan County's doughboy is one of only three known doughboys made of stone in the United States. (Courtesy of Morgan County Archives.)

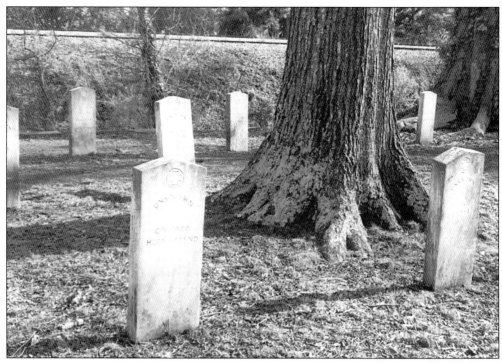

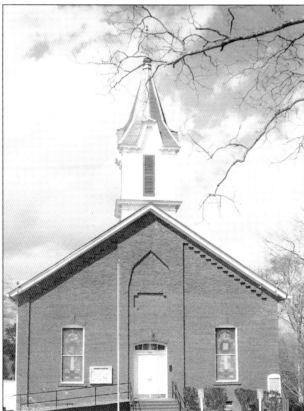

Buried with the unidentified Confederate soldiers in Madison Cemetery was an unidentified African American hospital attendant. The attendant worked at one of the Confederate hospitals in Madison. It is not known how he came to work in the hospital, though many African Americans were paid workers in Confederate hospitals. (Photograph by Marcia Brooks.)

Calvary Baptist Church is located on Academy Street. The Madison Baptist Church had its original building on this site, a wood-frame structure. African American members of Madison Baptist Church received letters of dismission in 1865 so they could form a church of their own. They formed the original congregation of Calvary Baptist Church. The current building was completed in 1883. (Photograph by Marcia Brooks.)

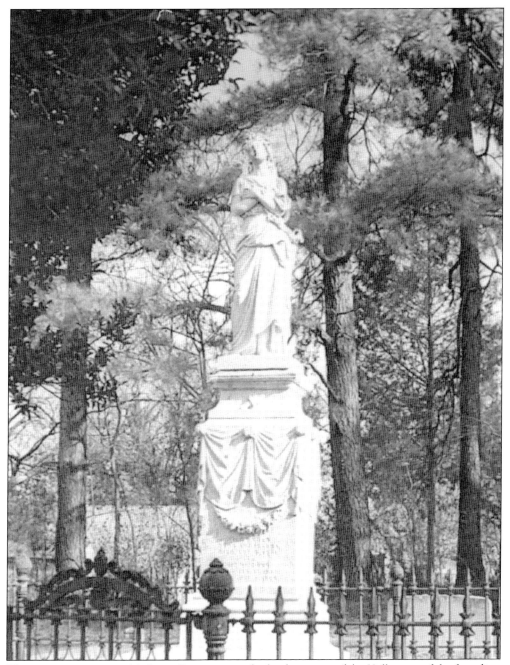

This poignant statue in Madison Cemetery overlooks the graves of the Kolbs, one of the founding families of Madison. An iron fence surrounds the family plot. Kolb Street in Madison is named for this prominent family. Wilds and Nancy Kolb built Boxwood in 1851. The pensive look on the face of the figure reflects the somber tones of the cemetery. (Photograph by Marcia Brooks.)

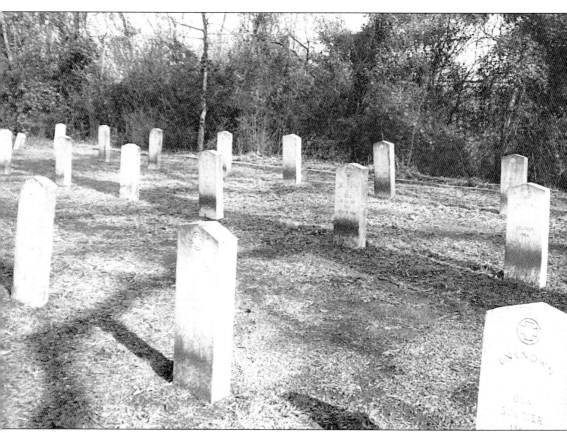

Graves of unidentified Confederate soldiers stand at attention in Madison Cemetery. A total of 51 unidentified soldiers are buried in this cemetery. No major battles occurred in the vicinity, but there were several hospitals in Madison during the Civil War. Unidentified soldiers who died in these hospitals were brought here for burial. (Photograph by Marcia Brooks.)

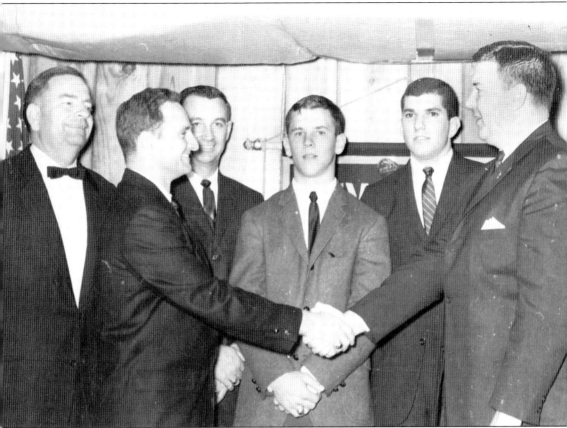

The Kiwanis Club honors the 1963 Morgan County Bulldog football team at a banquet in December 1963. Bill Cochran (right) congratulates head coach Jack Gnehm on an outstanding freshman season. Tom Riden (school principal, left) and Bill Corry (former head coach, third from left) look on. Also pictured are team cocaptains Candler Hunt (fourth from left) and Mike Lurey (fifth from left). Football in Madison has a long legacy of tradition. Riden played football for Madison High School in 1935, which was when the school had one of its best teams. He received a work-sports scholarship to Piedmont College in 1936. After graduating from Piedmont, he obtained a master's of education in school administration from the University of Georgia. Corry, or "Coach Corry" as he is affectionately known, also attended Piedmont and obtained a specialist in education degree from the University of Georgia. He coached the Morgan County High School state championship teams of 1955, 1958, 1959, and 1962. In 1963, he entered school administration. (Courtesy of Morgan County Archives.)

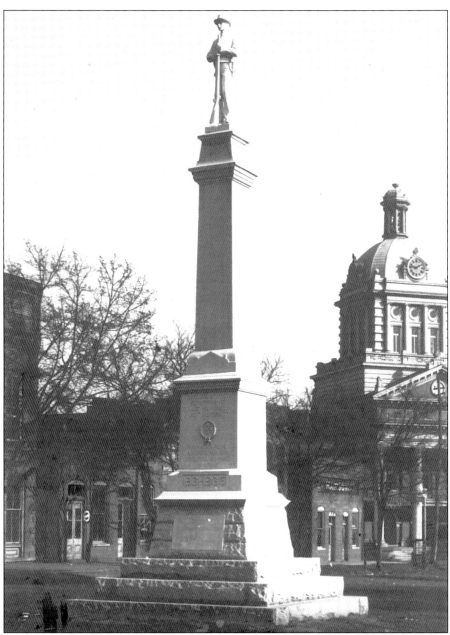

Madison's Confederate monument is pictured in 1910 on East Jefferson Street near the corner of Main Street. The statue was erected by the Morgan County Chapter of the United Daughters of the Confederacy in memory of those who died during the Civil War. The monument was erected in 1908 and dedicated on January 5, 1909. The current courthouse stands in the background. The office of the *Madisonian* can be seen at the corner of Hancock and East Jefferson Streets. Part of Madison City Hall can be seen on the left side of the picture. This monument was moved to Hill Park on South Main Street in 1955. In 1919, the land for Hill Park was donated by (Isabella) Belle Hill Knight, daughter of Sen. Joshua Hill, and it became the first city park. Belle was born October 27, 1853, and died August 8, 1938. She married Dr. Gazaway B. Knight, captain of the Panola Guards, Cobb's Legion. (Photograph by Marcia Brooks.)

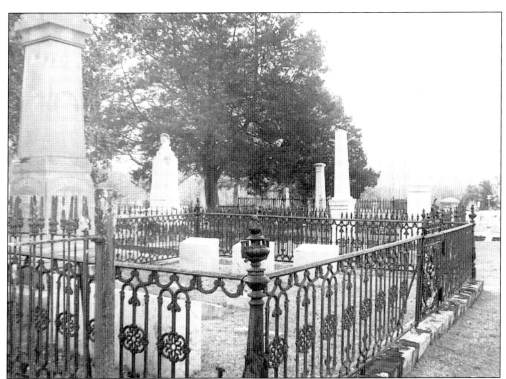

Ornate ironwork surrounds some of the older graves in the Madison Cemetery. Although ironwork is not a common architectural feature on the buildings of Morgan County, it was used to surround quite a few plots in the cemetery. The original train line in Madison passes through the cemetery, dividing the old and new sections. (Photograph by Marcia Brooks.)

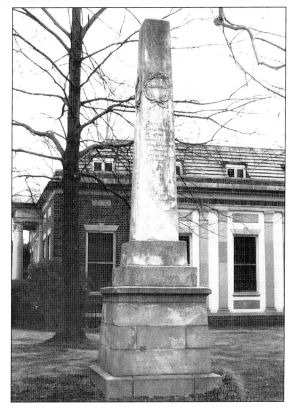

Benjamin Braswell, an early benefactor of Morgan County, died in 1817. In his will, he provided for a fund for indigent children in the county for schoolbooks, materials, and some clothing. Soon, the widows were coming to Morgan County to benefit from this resource, which in turn made education an important factor in Madison early in its history. The justices of the inferior court placed this monument on the square in Madison to honor the original benefactor, Benjamin Braswell. (Photograph by Marcia Brooks.)

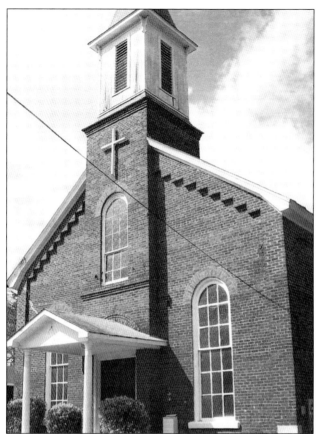

St. Paul African Methodist Episcopal Church was built in 1881. It is located on Fifth Street in the Canaan area of Madison. The land for the church was granted by Anna G. Johnston in 1871. Professions of early church members included barbers, brick masons, carpenters, caterers, doctors, farmers, funeral directors, janitors, musicians, politicians, shoemakers, and teachers. (Photograph by Marcia Brooks.)

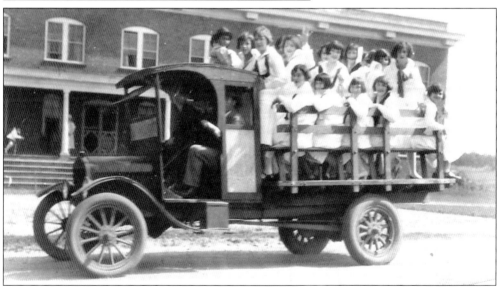

Students from Madison A&M are seen loading up to go to church in the 1920s. Attendance in church would have been a regular part of the student's life at the A&M boarding school. The students would have attended local churches, perhaps the same ones that schoolteachers and administrators belonged to. (Courtesy of Morgan County High School.)

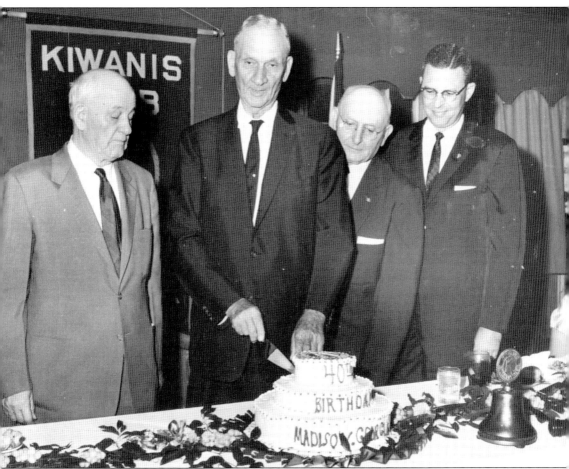

The Kiwanis Club celebrates its 40th birthday in Madison in 1962. Madison's chapter, one of the 10 oldest in Georgia, was founded on September 5, 1922. Even though the Kiwanis Club International did not officially allow women to join until 1987, to comply with a Supreme Court decision, Emily Carpenter joined the Madison Kiwanis Club in the 1930s. She was one of its most active members. Three charter members of the Madison Chapter, C.R. Mason, F.C. Newton, and E.G. Atkinson, are pictured with Pres. George R. Cochran Jr. The Kiwanis Club organizes many civic and community projects. The picnic shelter in Hill Park is one of the many projects the organization has worked on in Madison. The club has held its meetings at the Brady Inn since 1988. A plaque bearing the name of all past presidents of the Madison chapter hangs in the inn. (Courtesy of Morgan County Archives.)

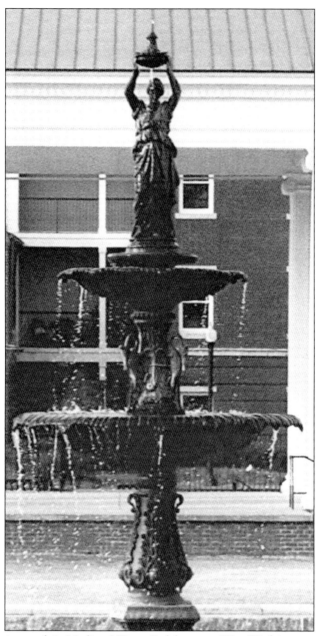

The Cooke Fountain stands in Madison's Town Park between West Washington and West Jefferson Streets. The current iron fountain is a replica of an original fountain made of zinc and given to the town by resident Sarah Cooke, a Northern lady who moved to Madison after losing her husband and son in the Civil War. The town clock and the first library for the schools were also bequeathed to the town by Sarah upon her death. The original fountain was cast by the J.L. Mott Company in 1908 and stood in the street at the intersection of East Jefferson and Hancock Streets. When the street was paved, it was moved to the center of the town square and later removed when the post office was built in 1931. Only the Grecian maiden that perched atop the original fountain remains. It can be seen at Heritage Hall, home of the Morgan County Historical Society, on South Main Street. The current fountain was cast by Robinson Iron. (Photograph by Marcia Brooks.)

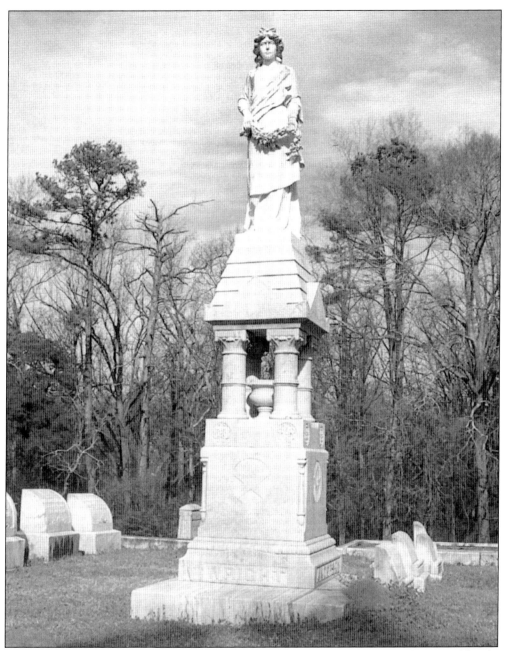

This statue stands in a quiet corner of Madison Cemetery. The cemetery is divided into an old and a new portion. The earliest known burial in the old section is from 1811. Early settlers of Madison made a decision to bury their loved ones in a collective cemetery rather than in separate denominational ones. But just as they were segregated in life, so were African Americans segregated from whites in death. Various areas of the cemetery were "laid out" or set aside for African Americans. Whites did not bury their dead in these areas, and African Americans did not bury their dead in the white sections. Over time, the cemetery has expanded to encompass four different areas. One of the areas was originally a private cemetery set up for whites only. The city bought this cemetery in 1979 and removed the restrictive covenants. (Photograph by Marcia Brooks.)

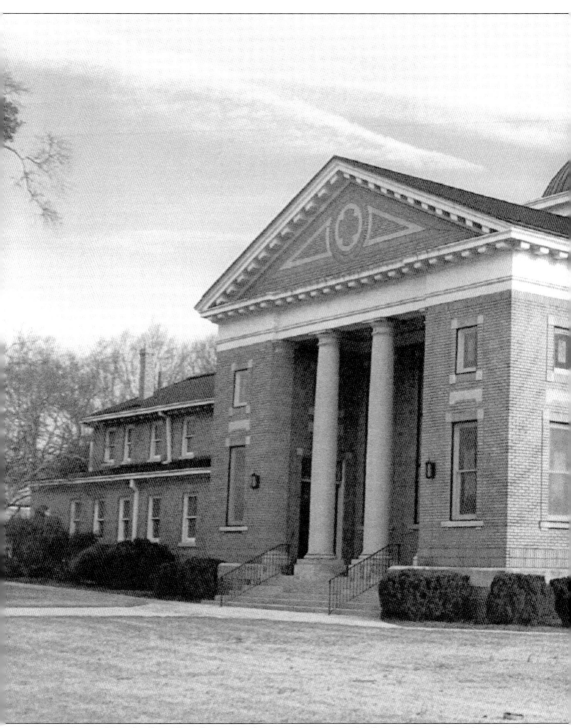

First United Methodist Church on South Main Street was built in 1914 in the Akron style of architecture. The church was founded in 1807. The first church building was erected in 1808 at an unknown location. The lot where the present-day Episcopal Advent Church stands on Academy Street was granted to the church by the Georgia legislature in 1825. A white, wood-

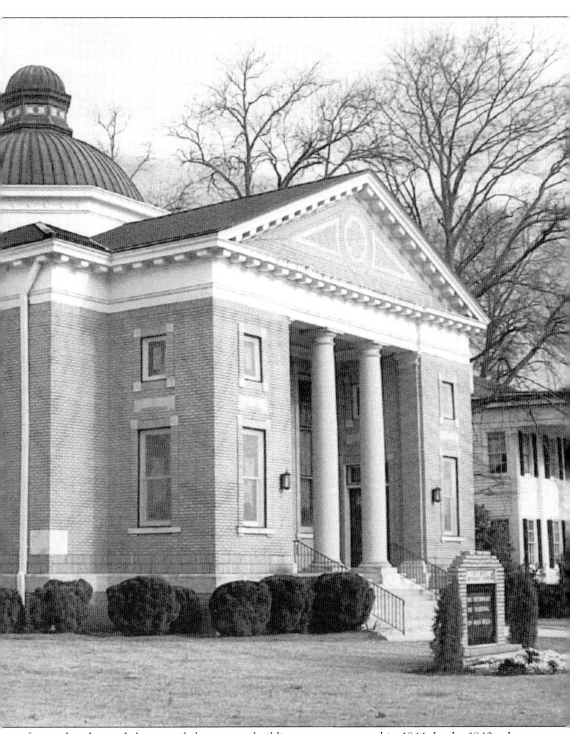

frame church stood there until the present building was constructed in 1844. In the 1840s, the church was considered one of the largest and finest in the state, and the Georgia Conference met in Madison. Madison brick mason Harold L. Murray worked on the design and construction of this building. (Photograph by Marcia Brooks.)

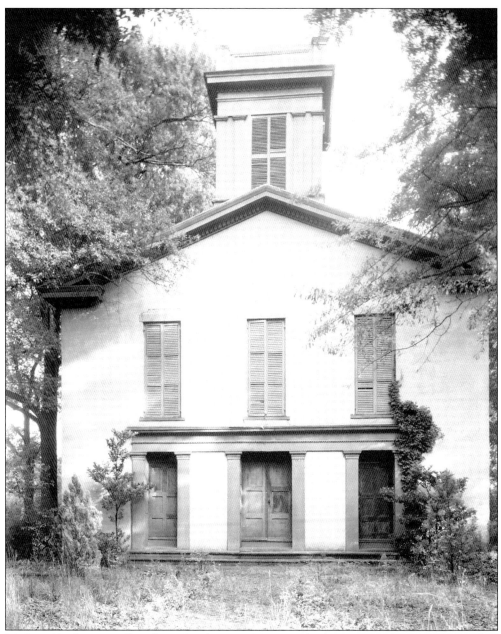

Madison Presbyterian Church on South Main Street was built in 1842. The congregation had organized in 1821 and held services in the courthouse and in the Madison Male Academy prior to construction of the present building. The church is a simplified Greek Revival design, built by Daniel Killion, a master builder. It was erected on property known as the Weston tract. At the time of the purchase, the property was occupied by Jacob E. Role and included a house, carriage shop, and blacksmith shop. In 1908, Elizabeth Speed donated seven Tiffany windows. The church originally had a slave gallery that had an outside entrance. In 1866, Ellen Axson, who was the daughter of the church's pastor, became the future president Woodrow Wilson's first wife. A silver tea service belonging to the church was stolen by a Union soldier during the Civil War but was later returned. (Courtesy of the Library of Congress.)

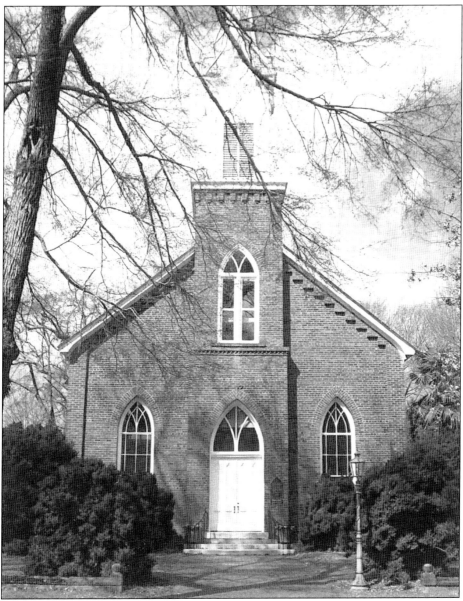

The Episcopal Advent Church on Academy Street was built in 1844 in the Gothic Revival style as a Methodist church. Madison's Episcopal congregation purchased it in 1961. Before this, the building had served as the town's early Methodist church and as a Christian Science church. The church was renovated in 1961 and consecrated by Madison's Episcopal congregation in 1963. The building contains an original slave gallery, which now serves as the church's organ loft. The vesper bells can still be heard in the evenings. Prior to 1848, the Episcopal congregation met in the courthouse and private residences. The original Episcopal church was located in the southeast corner of Madison Cemetery, built on property deeded to them by the Madison Male Academy. The diminutive Greek Revival chapel seated 40 people. As homeless and destitute people sought refuge in it, the building deteriorated in the 1930s. The property was deconsecrated on May 3, 1937, and sold to the City of Madison for $250. The city razed the building and sold cemetery plots where it once stood. (Photograph by Marcia Brooks.)

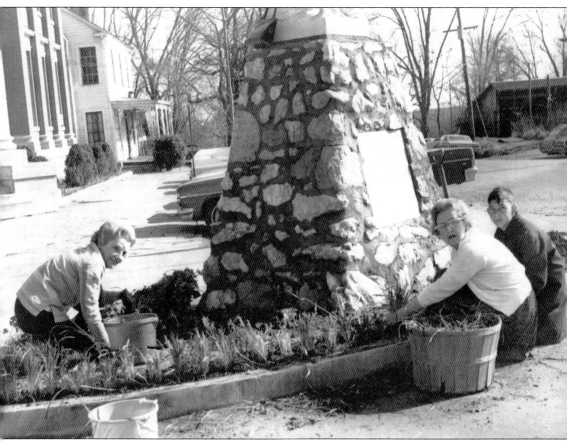

Laura "Polly" Weihe Newton (left) and Mrs. W.L. Gardner (center) plant greenery around the doughboy statue in front of the Morgan County Courthouse in January 1970 with an unidentified boy. Newton was regent of the Henry Walton Chapter of the Daughters of the American Revolution (DAR). The DAR gave the greenery to the town. The Henry Walton Chapter of the DAR has a long history of service to the community of Madison. The chapter was organized on March 2, 1910. The first officers were Sue Reid Walton Manley, regent; Kittie Fitzpatrick, vice regent; Lula Atkinson, recording secretary; Mary Walton Trammell Newton, corresponding secretary; Lula Holland, treasurer; Bessie Walton, registrar; and Anna Trammell, historian. The chapter was named for Capt. Henry Walton, a Revolutionary War solider and the ancestor of several of the charter members. (Courtesy of Morgan County Archives.)

Four

A LEGACY OF EDUCATION

Though Madison is best known for its beautiful historic homes and buildings, the town has also been a center of education since its early years. The first formal education offered in Morgan County was at the Madison Male Academy, established in 1815. The original building burned in 1824, and its replacement was funded by a lottery. Students studied Greek, Latin, geography, grammar, arithmetic, reading, and writing.

In the mid-1800s, Madison became home to several academies. Two female colleges opened. These colleges attracted students from all over the country, offering a classical education for young ladies. Throughout the 1800s, many private schools for girls were opened. After the Civil War, the first public school commissioners were elected, introducing the era of public schools in Madison and Morgan County. Many of the private schools were brought under the public school system at this time. Madison was one of the first locations to offer educational opportunities to free slaves. But, like the rest of the south, schools in Madison were segregated until the mid-1960s.

In the early 1900s, Madison was chosen as one of Georgia's agriculture and mechanical school sites. Madison A&M was a boarding school, and students attended from counties throughout the district. The City of Madison infrastructure was extended to the location one mile east of town to provide water, lights, and sewage. After the A&M schools closed in the 1930s, the campus served as a National Youth Association facility for a period of time, then became the home of Morgan County High School in the late 1940s. The other schools in the county consolidated in the 1960s, around the same time that schools were integrated. In recent years, Morgan County schools in Madison have been recognized as among the best in the state of Georgia. The legacy begun in the early 1800s continues.

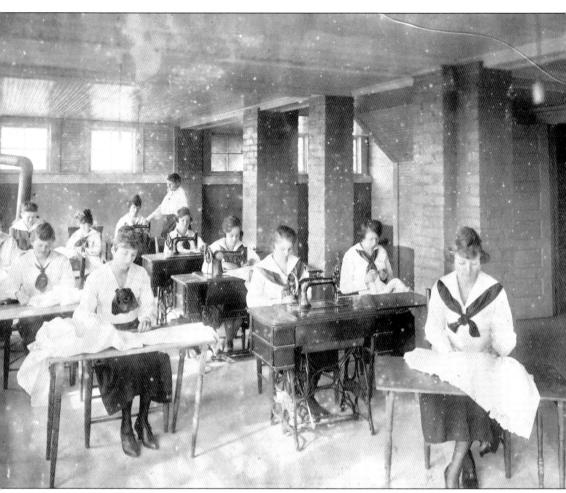

Some students have their own sewing machines in this sewing class at Madison A&M. Others work at tables cutting cloth from patterns. An instructor circulates, pausing to observe a student at the back of the classroom. For many years, homemaking skills were taught in the schools in home economics. There was also a school organization called the Future Homemakers of America. However, the training in classes was intended to do more than just prepare a young lady for marriage and a family. These young ladies were expected to learn a vocation, such as dress designing. The girls wore uniforms resembling sailor outfits. Just as in a typing class, not all the sewing machines were made by the same company. One Singer sewing machine can be seen, but the others bear a different brand name. (Courtesy of Morgan County High School.)

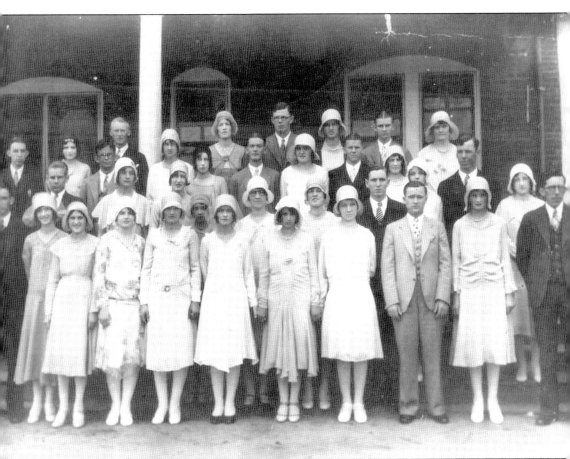

The Madison A&M class of 1930 is pictured. In spite of the positive impact the Madison A&M School had on the community and on the students, an effort to reorganize higher education in Georgia was initiated by Gov. L.G. Hardman. The restructuring of public colleges and universities in the state meant the end of the A&M schools statewide. In 1931, the Reorganization Act was passed by the Georgia General Assembly. This act created the Board of Regents of the University System of Georgia. The school was originally administratively attached to the College of Agriculture at the University of Georgia, and funding came from the Georgia Department of Agriculture. The act placed the A&M schools under the control of the newly created board, which promptly abolished the schools. The last class of Madison A&M would graduate in 1933. After commencement exercises in 1933, the school was closed. (Courtesy of Morgan County High School.)

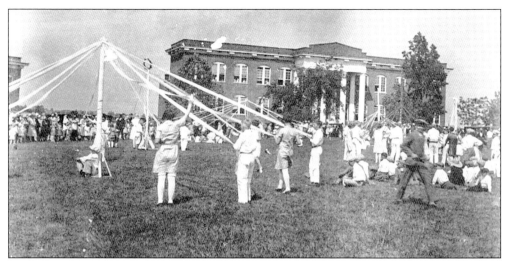

Students gather around a maypole on the front campus of Madison A&M. The school was located on a hill near town. The campus included dorms, workshops, barns, orchards, pastures, and sports areas. This school, and the others in Georgia like it, was established through the efforts of Gov. Joseph Terrell, then known as "the education governor." (Courtesy of Morgan County High School.)

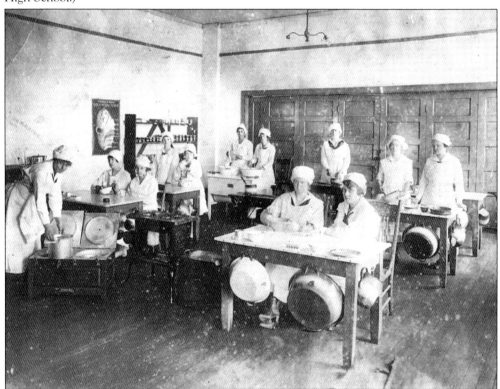

Students look up from their worktables in a cooking class at Madison A&M. The classroom contains its own stove in addition to a variety of cooking implements. This was a unique boarding school that offered agricultural education, liberal arts, and vocational training, along with competitive sports programs. All of the original buildings are now gone. (Courtesy of Morgan County High School.)

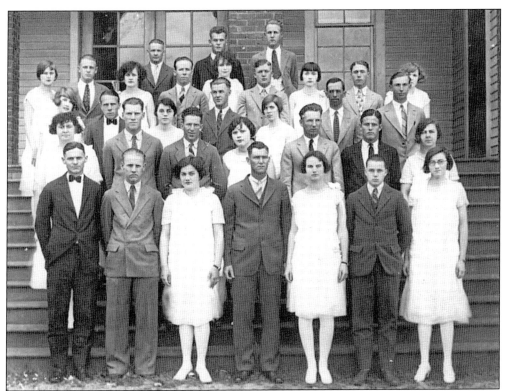

The Madison A&M class of 1926 is pictured above. The previous year, the graduating class constructed the brick pillars at the center entrance to the campus. Subsequent classes would construct the pillars that stand at the other two entrances. The boys outnumbered the girls in this class by almost a 2:1 ratio. (Courtesy of Morgan County High School.)

Students at Madison A&M are pictured constructing a silo on the campus. Georgia had a dozen agricultural preparatory boarding schools, one of which was Madison A&M. Very unique, it was neither wholly high school or vocational, but it gave students a wide range of training, liberal arts education, and athletic programs. (Courtesy of Morgan County High School.)

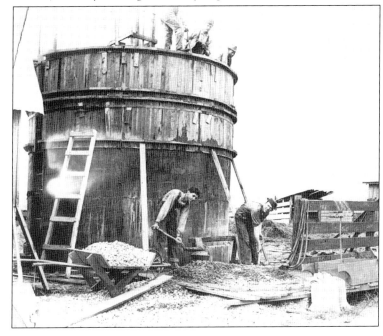

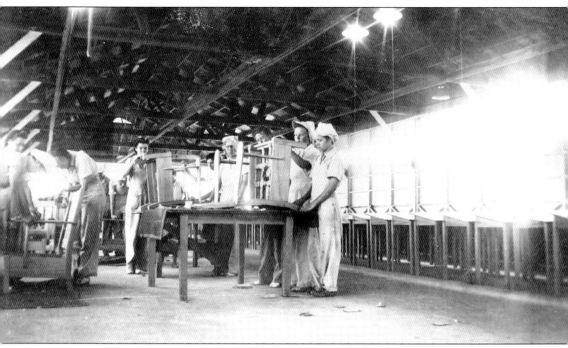

In this photograph, female National Youth Administration (NYA) participants work on construction of wooden chairs on the former Madison A&M campus. The vacated campus was used by the NYA for about 10 years beginning in 1935. The NYA was similar to the Civilian Conservation Corps (CCC) in that it provided work for the unemployed during the 1930s–1940s. However, unlike the CCC, the NYA allowed females to participate. (Courtesy of Morgan County High School.)

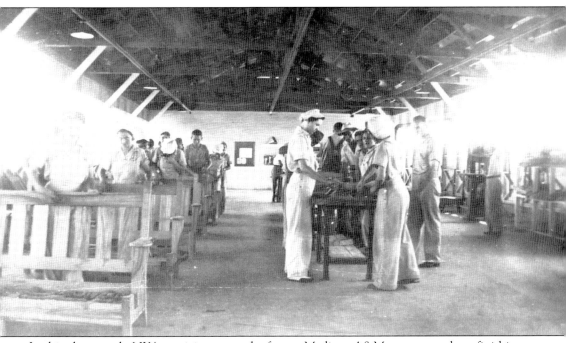

In this photograph, NYA participants on the former Madison A&M campus work on finishing wooden benches on the left, while others work at tables. NYA programs provided work for young men and women not in school and taught them various skills. On the job training included construction trades, metal and woodworking, office work, recreation, and health care. Participants also worked in parks, national forests, and outdoor recreation areas. (Courtesy of Morgan County High School.)

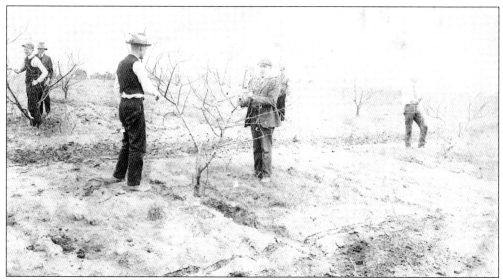

Students at Madison A&M are pictured pruning peach trees in an orchard located on the campus. The schools offered a wide selection of training to acquire useful skills, much of which is still offered in today's curriculum. Students learned many things that would help them make a living or choose a vocation. (Courtesy of Morgan County High School.)

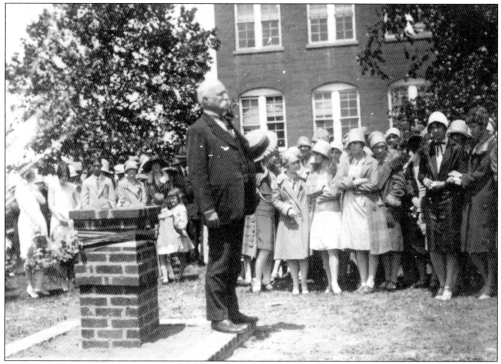

Col. E.W. Butler was the president of Madison A&M. During organization and construction of the school in Madison, he served as treasurer, handling construction funds. The Madison A&M buildings were designed by famous Atlanta architect Haralson Bleckley, and all the campuses in Georgia were identical. At the time, Madison A&M served 12 counties in the Eighth Congressional District. (Courtesy of Morgan County High School.)

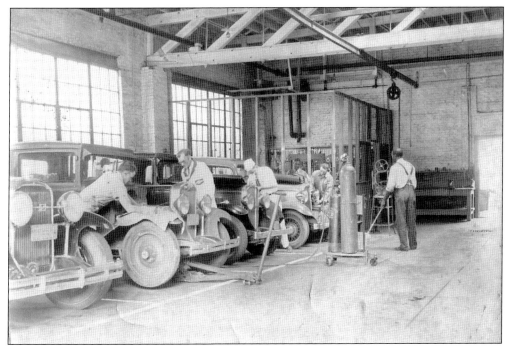

Students are seen working in the auto shop at Madison A&M. Citizens sometimes donated old cars, trucks, tractors, or machinery to the school for use in training students to become skilled mechanics. These skills were valuable assets to the students and to the communities they lived in. The second man from the left appears to be an observer or trainer from Chevrolet. (Courtesy of Morgan County High School.)

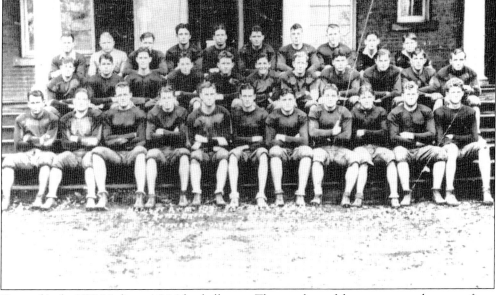

Pictured is the 1931 Madison A&M football team. The members of the team sat on the steps of one of the school buildings for this photograph. In each of the previous two years, the team won the North Georgia Football Championship. Both years, they were defeated at the state championship by Georgia Military College. (Courtesy of Morgan County High School.)

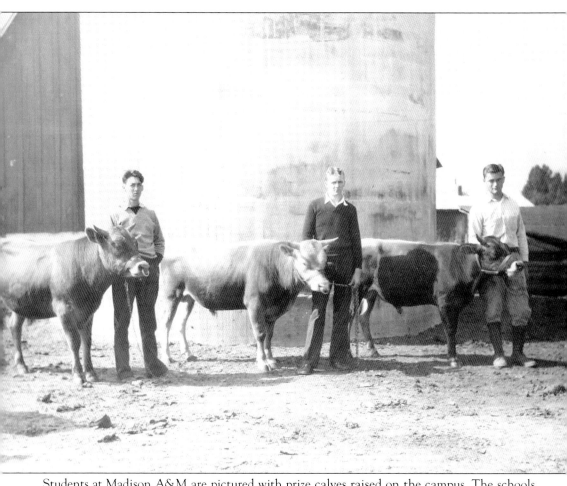

Students at Madison A&M are pictured with prize calves raised on the campus. The schools organized clubs such as the 4-H and Future Farmers of America to encourage students and help them learn with projects that were entered in shows and fairs for prizes. Agriculture has always been, and still is, a vital economic force in Madison and Morgan County. (Courtesy of Morgan County High School.)

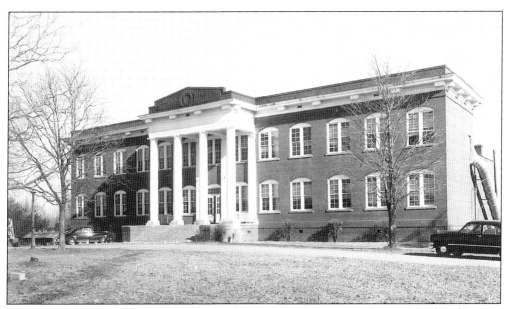

The main building at Morgan County High School is shown around 1950. The building was on the campus of what was originally the Eighth District Agriculture and Mechanical School (colloquially known as Madison A&M). The building remained on the campus until 1963, when it was razed in order to construct a new building. (Courtesy of Morgan County High School.)

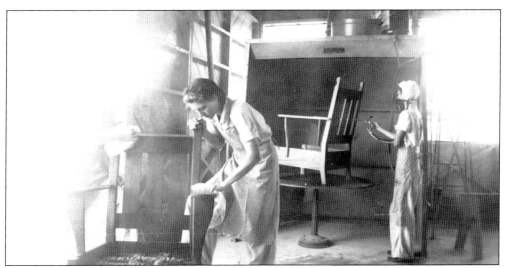

During the years from 1935 to 1945, the Madison A&M campus was used by the NYA for construction activities. The furniture shop shown was newly constructed. In these facilities, youth built furniture to send to Georgia's military bases to support the war effort. NYA participants are shown above building furniture. (Courtesy of Morgan County High School.)

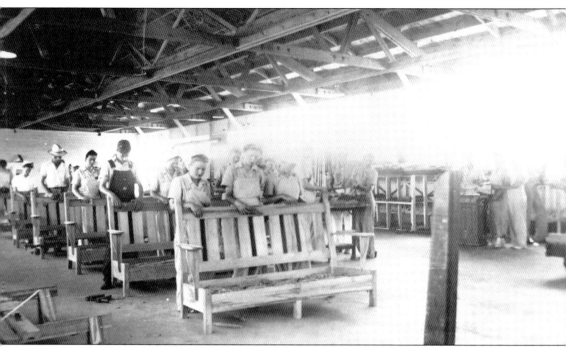

In this photograph, NYA participants are shown finishing wooden benches. It appears that this was a coeducational facility. The Depression of the 1930s had created a huge surplus of young people out of work. The NYA was a New Deal program designed to provide young people, ages 16 to 24, with training and skills, while being paid to learn. Most participants lived at home. The program was targeted to those youth who were not in school. (Courtesy of Morgan County High School.)

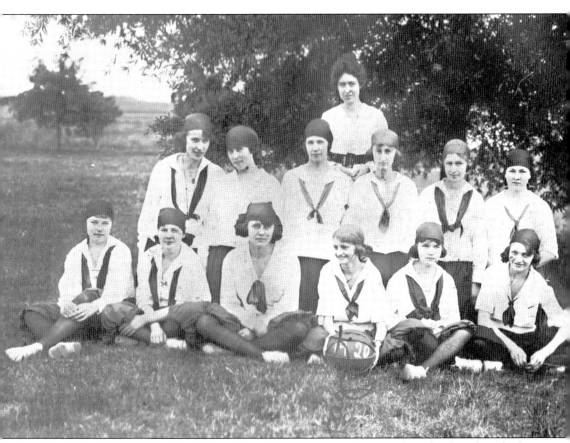

The Madison A&M girls' basketball team poses around 1930. To get into this school, students had to be of good character, have very good references, and possess above-average abilities. Every student had to work—the boys worked on the farms, and the girls preserved, prepared, and served food. Girls also learned secretarial skills, homemaking, and bookkeeping. The instruction at the school was far ahead of its time. Fully accredited, it was a Group 1 four-year high school. Group 1 high schools were classified by the Georgia Department of Education as "the best schools in teaching staff, equipment of laboratory, library, and building." Vocational and liberal arts training, teacher certification programs, and extension education were all offered at Madison A&M School. The courses prepared students for college, provided advanced technical training in many fields, and assured they could enter the workforce upon graduation. During the 25 years of operation, many shops, outbuildings, barns, and facilities were constructed. Classrooms and laboratories were all state of the art by contemporary standards. (Courtesy of Morgan County High School.)

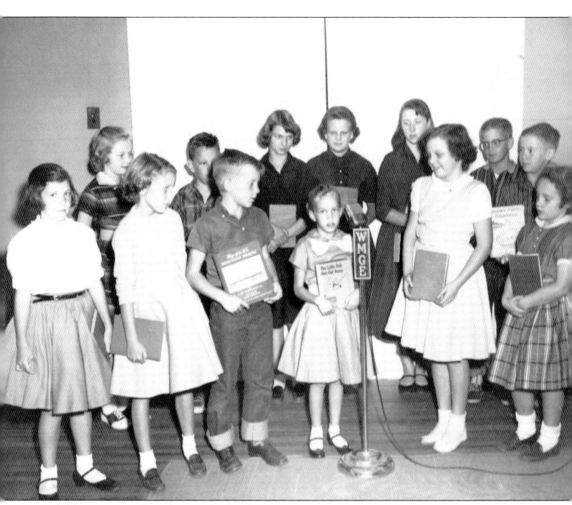

Children present their favorite books during story time at WMGE, Madison's radio station, in December 1957. The program was presented live at 9:30 a.m. on a Saturday. It was sponsored by the Jasper-Morgan-Putnam County Library (later named the Uncle Remus Regional Library). The children are, from left to right, (first row) Janet Lewis and Ann Lawrence from Eatonton, John Paul Martin from Madison, Alice Prevatt from Monticello, and June Beth Thornton and Jean Burge from Madison; (second row) Belle Hewitt and Stevie Griffith from Eatonton; Jean Calvert, Jane Booth, and Barbara Shockley from Madison; Andrew Marshall from Eatonton, and Joe Hayes from Madison. Featured books included *The Little Fish That Got Away*, *Ships of the US Merchant Marine*, and *Rocky Point Campers*. The program featured students from all three counties served by the library at the time. The regional library system name comes from Joel Chandler Harris's tales related by the character Uncle Remus. Joel Chandler Harris was born in neighboring Putnam County on December 9, 1848. (Courtesy of Morgan County Library.)

The main building at Madison A&M was later used by the high school when it relocated to the campus. The building had two or three stories with wooden oiled floors, large windows, and fire escapes for the upper floors. Classes were conducted in this building until the end of 1962. It was razed in 1963 to make way for more modern buildings. (Courtesy of Morgan County High School.)

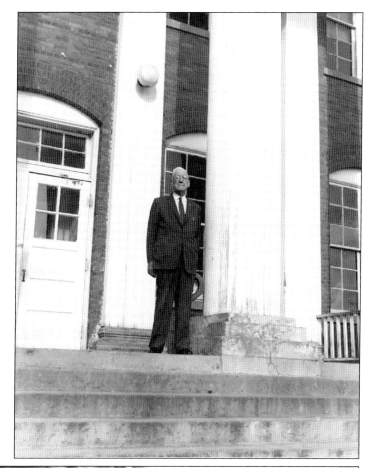

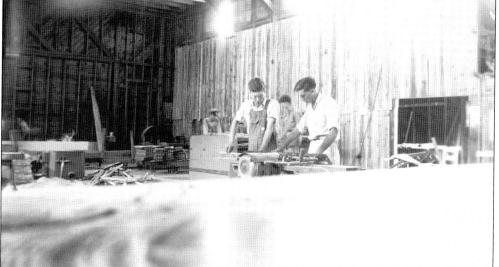

In this photograph, NYA participants on the former Madison A&M campus use equipment to prepare wood for construction projects. It was during the NYA period of the campus that the first of the original A&M buildings was razed. (Courtesy of Morgan County High School.)

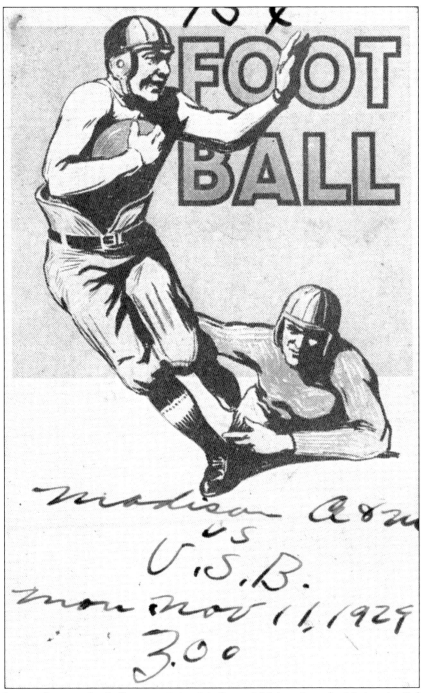

Pictured is a ticket to a football game pitting Madison A&M against the University School for Boys (Atlanta) on November 11, 1929. A lasting tradition of championship high school football teams in Morgan County began with the Madison A&M Aggies. Legendary University of Georgia football coach Wallace "Wally" Butts began his coaching career here, leading the team to victory in the GIAA North Georgia Football Championship in 1929 and 1930. (Courtesy of Morgan County High School.)

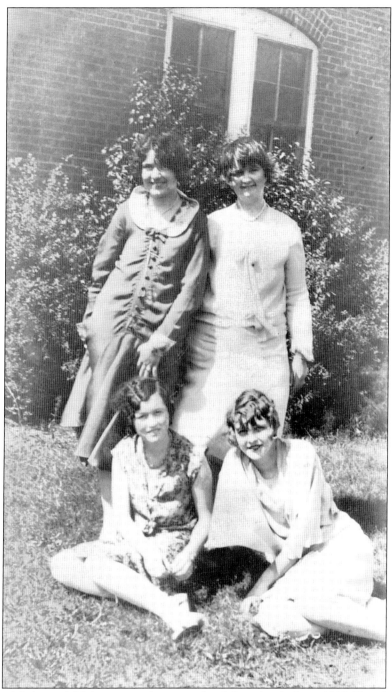

Students at Madison A&M pose on the grounds of the school about 1929. Female students attending the school were expected to learn skills leading to careers, such as school dieticians, clothes designers, hygienists, and public health workers. Evening and weekend activities for male and female students included attending concerts, learning to play musical instruments, participating in debates in the two literary societies, and developing skills at social functions. (Courtesy of Morgan County High School.)

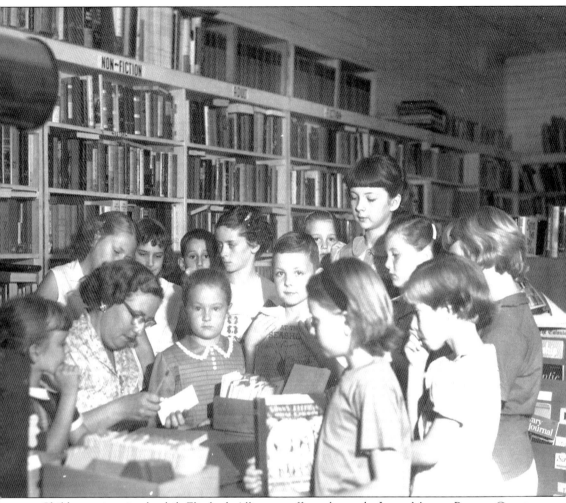

Children wait patiently while Elizabeth Alliston, staff member at the Jasper-Morgan-Putnam County Library in Madison, checks out books. The library was located in the Madison Graded School in the 1950s, when this photograph was taken. The Madison Graded School was built in 1895. It now houses the Madison-Morgan Cultural Center. (Courtesy of Morgan County Library.)

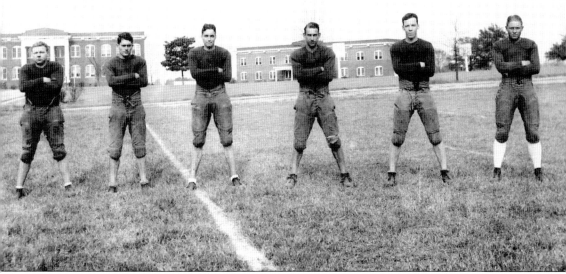

In this photograph, football players pose on the front lawn of Madison A&M in the early 1930s. The year 2007 marked the 100th anniversary of the Eighth District Agricultural and Mechanical School in Madison. Georgia governor Joseph Terrell had a vision for a different kind of school, and for 25 years, the youth of Morgan County and 11 other counties in the district reaped the benefits of this unique education. In 1906, Madison A&M and the other schools like it were established. There were 12 Congressional Districts, and every district had one of these schools. This was an era when there were few accredited schools. Students were still attending one-room schools with all ages in one classroom. The A&M schools were created to satisfy a growing need for more specialized educational opportunities. (Courtesy of Morgan County High School.)

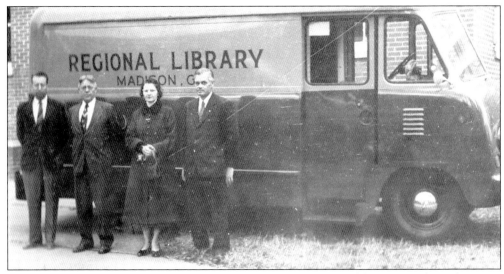

Pictured are, from left to right, Maurice Thompson, Custer Crawford (superintendent of Morgan County schools), Caroline H. Candler Hunt (chair of the library board), and Kay Tipton. They are commemorating the arrival of the Jasper-Morgan-Putnam County Library's new bookmobile on November 13, 1953. It was a big event, and children were excited when the bookmobile arrived. It was taken to each school, some churches, and even some homes in the days before the schools were consolidated. (Courtesy of the Morgan County Library.)

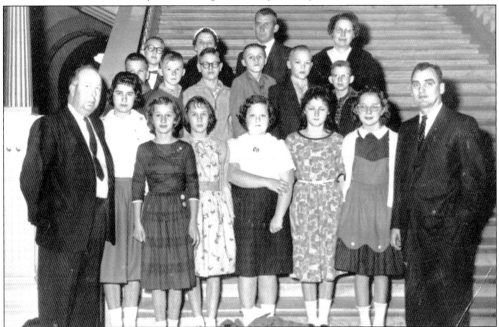

Children in seventh grade at Rutledge Elementary visit the Georgia State Capitol in Atlanta in February 1962, accompanied by Representatives Howard Tamplin (left) and Roy Lambert (right), Georgia state legislators from Madison. Tamplin served as a representative from 1949 to 1963. Lambert served as a senator from 1954 to 1958 and as a representative from 1962 to 1984. After the county's schools were consolidated, Rutledge Elementary was closed and all students attended schools in Madison. (Courtesy of Morgan County Archives.)

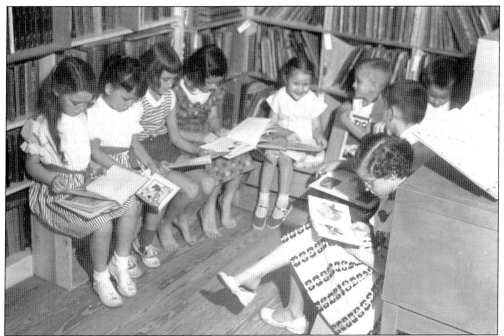

Schoolchildren sit in a corner of the Jasper-Morgan-Putnam County Library reading books in the 1950s. The library was located in the building that housed the Madison-Morgan Cultural Center from 1947 to 1974. Library staff and patrons constantly dealt with the struggles of inadequate space while located here. In 1974, the library relocated to a new facility on East Avenue. (Courtesy of Morgan County Library.)

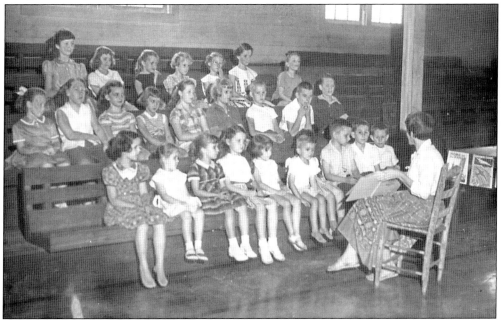

Grace Thompson, a library staff member, reads to children during storytelling hour in the former Madison Graded School gym in the 1950s. There was inadequate space to conduct this activity in the library, hence it was moved to the gym. (Courtesy of Morgan County Library.)

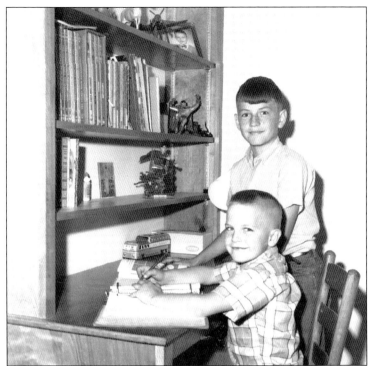

Fifth grader Neal Phelps helps his younger brother Gary with homework. This photograph was included in a supplement to the *Madisonian* in May 1967 extolling the virtues of electric power. (Courtesy of Morgan County Archives.)

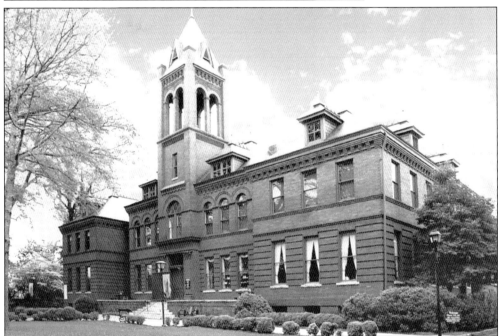

The Madison-Morgan Cultural Center on South Main Street was constructed in 1895 as one of the first graded public schools in the South. The building is in the Romanesque Revival style and houses an 1895 schoolroom museum, a beautiful auditorium for concerts and other events, and space for art exhibits. The original school bell still rings for visitors. (Courtesy of Morgan County Heritage website.)

Five

MADISON'S HOMES AND GARDENS

A leisurely stroll through Madison reveals why the town is internationally known for its homes and gardens. For a stretch of about one mile on each side of the center of town, historic homes line the streets. Each home has its own story to tell, some with ghosts to tell those tales. Some are famous for their beauty; others are not so famous but still as beautiful.

Although Madison is best known for its grand antebellum mansions, these actually represent a small fraction of the architectural styles on display. The town was incorporated in 1809, and the homes represent a variety of architectural styles that were popular during the town's first 100 years.

Homes dating from the early 19th century display simple styles, such as the Piedmont Plain plan and the Federal plan. Toward the mid-1800s, trends in architecture in Madison followed those of other areas of the South, and this was when the antebellum style reached its prominence. Following the Civil War, homes were built in a variety of styles, including Italianate, Victorian, and blended styles such as the front-gable side-wing style, that became very popular in the town.

The gardens of Madison are its hidden treasure. A number of homes have boxwood gardens on their property. Azaleas, irises, camellias, and hydrangeas also abound. Although most blooming plants slumber in the cold months, the stark beauty of the bare trees provides a serene backdrop for holiday festivities.

Madison opens its homes and gardens to visitors in May and December of each year. During these tours, visitors are able to experience the bounty of each season in the second largest historic district in Georgia. The people of Madison are its soul, but its homes and gardens are its heart. Along with the churches, monuments, and businesses, they are Madison—the No. 1 small town in America.

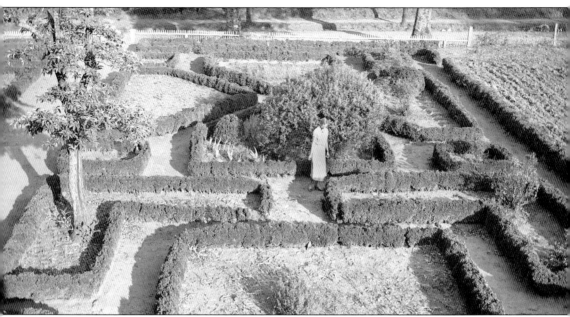

The boxwood hedges, placed in geometric designs to form a maze, are shown at Boxwood. The home has two facades, one on Academy Street and one on Old Post Road. A boxwood garden was placed on each side. The boxwoods are original to the homesite, but the architect of them is unidentified. Kittie Newton, former owner of the home, is shown in the garden. She was an early supporter of the conservation and preservation of the town's history. She also understood the appeal that Madison's homes would have to visitors. She organized Madison's first tour of homes in 1950 via an advertisement, which included her phone number. The boxwoods here are the ancestors of many others in the town of Madison. When Kittie trimmed the hedges every eight years or so, she would place an article in the newspaper advertising free cuttings to anyone who would come get them. (Courtesy of the Library of Congress.)

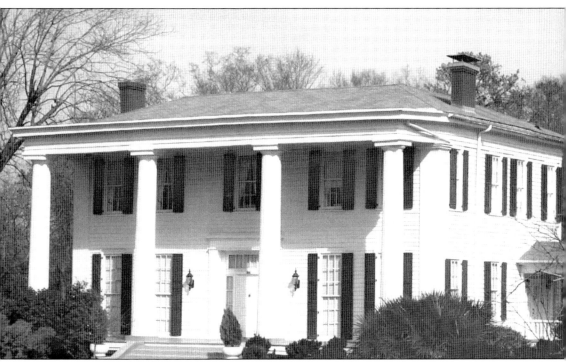

This Greek Revival home was built by Charles Mallory Irvin in 1851 using the central hall plan. Irvin was a Baptist minister and political leader. It later became the home of Charles and Frances Godfrey Candler. Charles was the son of Methodist bishop Warren Candler, who—along with brother Asa Griggs Candler, founder of the Coca-Cola Company—was instrumental in moving the main campus of Emory from Oxford to Atlanta. In the 1930s, the home was named Honeymoon by Sara Caroline "Carrie" Hardee Godfrey, after her old family home in Florida, which had hosted a young bridal couple. The garden in 1996 included many varieties of plants and some boxwoods said to be over 100 years old. The grounds at that time also included a smokehouse and slave quarters. It is located on Eatonton Road at the southern edge of Madison Historic District. (Courtesy of Marcia Brooks.)

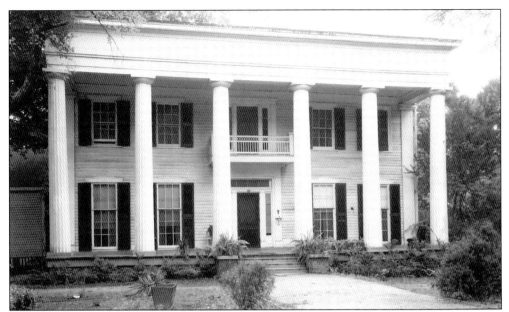

This photograph of the Martin-Baldwin-Weaver house from 1919 looks almost as if it could have been taken today. The home's basic appearance and character have been preserved. This photograph was part of the Carnegie Survey of the Architecture of the South. This, as well as many other homes in Madison, was photographed for this survey by Joel Benjamin Johnston in 1919. (Courtesy of the Library of Congress.)

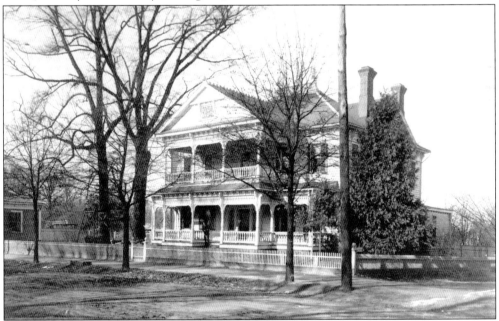

The Martin Richter House, built about 1905, stands on South Main Street in Madison across from the Chophouse Grill. The house is also known as the Dovecote House for its architecturally matching dovecote (a small structure used to house doves) located to the side of the house. The original home was of a much simpler style and was greatly embellished beginning in 1885 to its present Victorian appearance. (Courtesy of Morgan County Heritage website.)

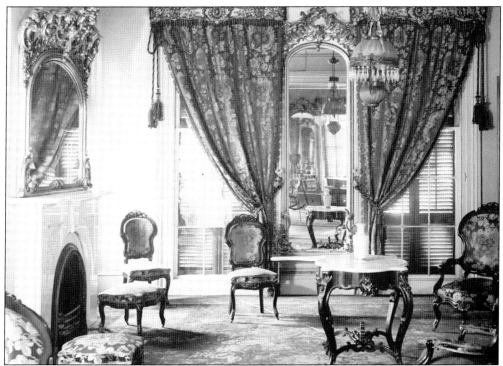

L.D. Andrew took this photograph of the parlor in the Kolb-Pou-Newton home in Madison, also known as Boxwood, on June 5, 1936. The furnishings and decor at the time were just as they had been when the house was built in 1851. Tall windows flank a mirror, which lightens the room and makes it appear bigger. The photographer's tripod camera can be seen reflected in the mirror. (Courtesy of the Library of Congress.)

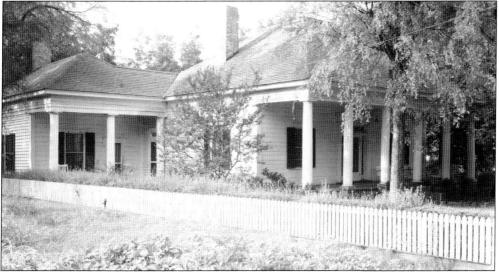

A side view of the Massey-Tipton-Bracewell House on North Main Street is shown in this photograph from about 1940. The photograph was taken by Frances Benjamin Johnston for the Carnegie Survey of the Architecture of the South. The Greek Revival cottage elements of the house are accentuated by the angle of the photograph. (Courtesy of the Library of Congress.)

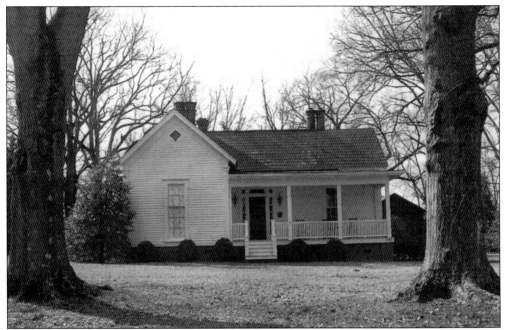

This home is on Eatonton Road at the southern edge of the historic district. Like many other cottages in Madison, this one was built in the front-gable side-wing style. However, its otherwise modest exterior includes an elaborate cutout in the gable and fancy chimneys. The simple porch railing offsets the ornate features, tempering what might otherwise be overpowering decoration. (Photograph by Marcia Brooks.)

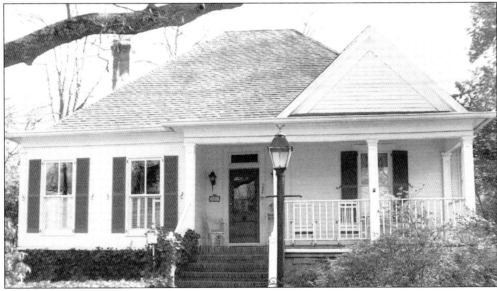

Fears Cottage on North Main Street was built around 1908. It is representative of the trend toward smaller homes in Southern towns in the years following the Civil War. The home is in the front-gable side-wing style with a hipped roof. Many post–World War II homes would follow this same basic pattern. (Photograph by Marcia Brooks.)

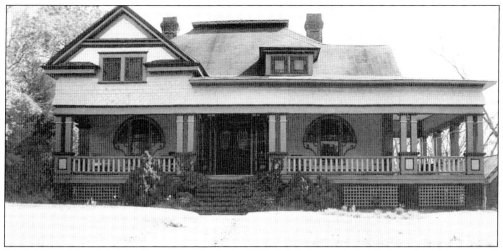

Iris Hill on North Main Street was built in 1853. This home is brightly colored in several coordinating shades. Stained-glass windows are encased in the intricately designed curved windows on the expansive front porch. The home has some features of the front-gable side-wing vernacular architectural style but actually predates the period of this type of design by almost 20 years. (Photograph by Marcia Brooks.)

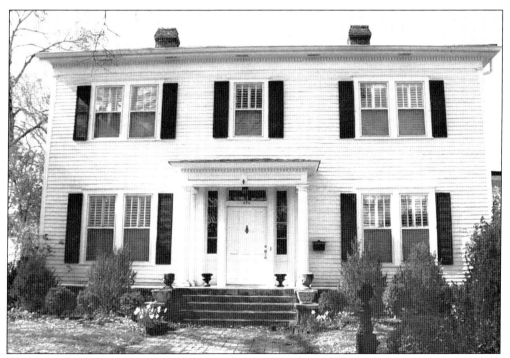

Pictured is the Foster-Thurmond House on South Main Street. This home was built in the 1890s and remodeled in the 1920s in the Colonial Revival style. The symmetry is typical of Georgian architecture, as is the pediment. However, the small entry porch also evokes Federal influences. Although Madison is best known for its antebellum mansions, they are far outnumbered by simpler homes such as this one. (Photograph by Marcia Brooks.)

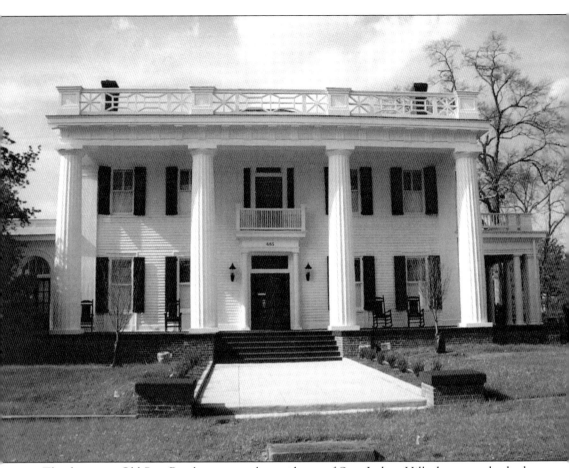

This home on Old Post Road was once the residence of Sen. Joshua Hill, the man who had a gentleman's agreement with General Sherman not to burn the homes of Madison during Sherman's march of destruction through Georgia. This agreement was reached when Hill met Sherman to claim the body of a deceased son who served with the Confederate army. Hill was elected to Congress in 1856, but being a staunch Unionist opposed to secession, he resigned from Congress in 1861 rather than vote for Georgia to secede from the Union. Hill was the mayor of Madison when Sherman's troops came through Georgia on their March to the Sea. He rode west to meet General Slocum to remind him of the arrangement that had been made. Although some buildings on the outskirts of town, including the depot and some warehouses, were burned, as well as some homes around the county, the homes of Madison were not torched by the Union troops. Hill was elected to the US Senate in 1868. (Photograph by Marcia Brooks.)

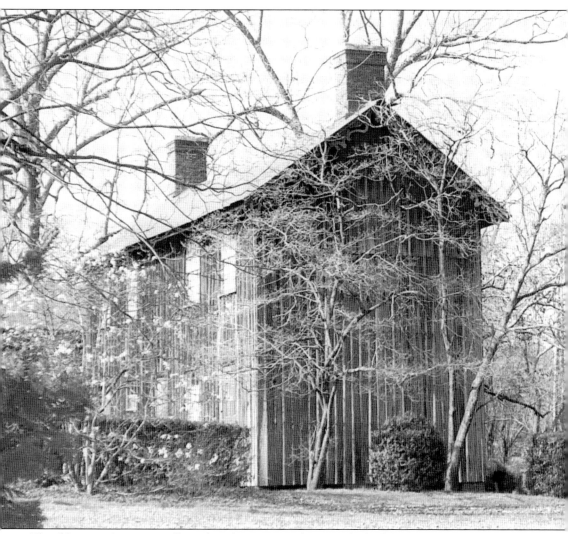

The old servants' quarters still stand on the property of Boxwood, which has entrances on Academy Street and Old Post Road. This building on the Old Post Road side was built at the same time as Boxwood—1851. Many of the large homes in Madison had external buildings such as this one on the grounds but very few remain. This building is unusual as far as servants' quarters go, being a two-story structure. It has three doors downstairs. The two doors on each end are entries to separate living quarters, indicating that two families of slaves probably lived in the building. The center door ascends to the second floor. The building was constructed in the Federal style, with twin chimneys. The absence of decorative elements also indicates the Federal style. Another building that stands behind this one served as a smokehouse. (Photograph by Marcia Brooks.)

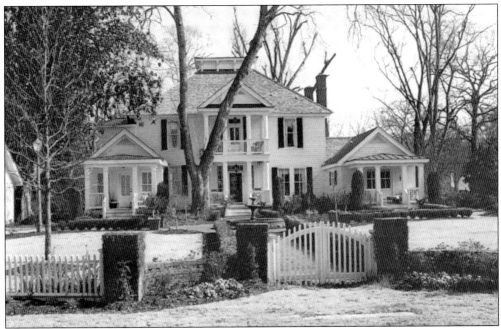

This view of the Paul and Lula Hurst Atkinson home was taken from Old Post Road. The other side of the home faces South Main Street and is shown on page 113. A number of houses in Madison have had entries on two streets over the years. South Main Street and Old Post Road run parallel and very close to each other, creating lots that have made this feasible. (Photograph by Marcia Brooks.)

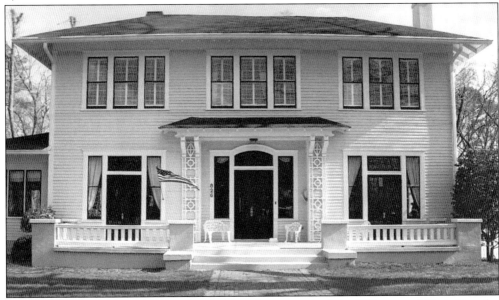

The Douglas-McDowell House on South Main Street was built by Tillman and Susie Douglas in 1917 on the site of an earlier house that burned. The home is a beautiful example of the Prairie-style architecture made popular by Frank Lloyd Wright. The home was later owned by R. Frank McDowell, one of the owners of McDowell Grocery Company on West Jefferson Street in Madison. (Courtesy of Marcia Brooks.)

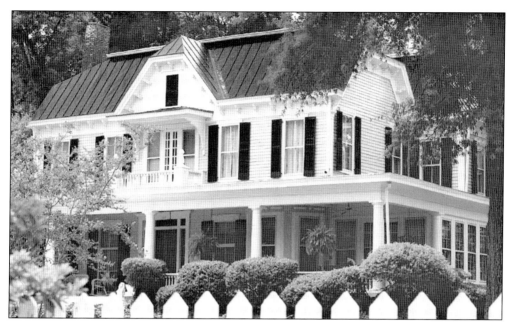

The Foster-Boswell House is located on Academy Street at the corner of Central Avenue. According to tradition, the current structure was built around a much earlier structure on the site. This home incorporates several architectural types harmoniously, including Georgian, Federal, and Greek Revival. This home features a uniquely shaped gable on the front. (Courtesy of Marcia Brooks.)

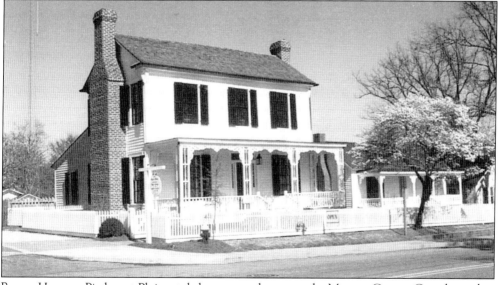

Rogers House, a Piedmont Plain–style home, stands next to the Morgan County Courthouse but predates it by almost 100 years. The home has had 17 different owners over the years. Adeline Rose, a woman who was born into slavery, built Rose Cottage, located to the right of the Rogers House in the picture, in 1891. Her home was originally on the south side of the Georgia Railroad right-of-way in east Madison. She earned her living by taking in washing and ironing at 50¢ a load. Much of her early work was done at the Hardy House, a hotel near the railroad depots in Madison, run by Oliver Hardy's mother. In 1966, the City of Madison moved Rose Cottage to its present location. (Courtesy of Morgan County Heritage website.)

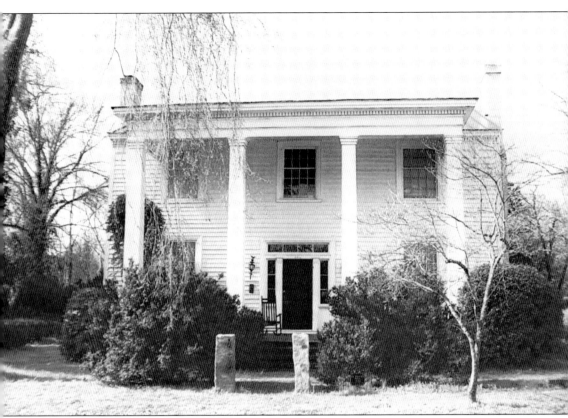

John Colbert built the Stagecoach Inn. The earliest part of the home dates to about 1810. It is believed that the original building was moved to the present site from another location. It stands on Old Post Road, originally known as South First Street. The street follows the path of the main stagecoach route from Charleston to New Orleans. The building served as an inn along the stagecoach route. The home originally had wings on each side. The wings were later moved to the side property and became guest homes. After stagecoach operation dwindled with the arrival of the railroad around 1840, the inn was used as a boardinghouse for teachers and students of Madison's private academies and two girls' colleges. In 1941, Cornelius "Neil" Vason Sr. purchased the home, giving it the Neil Vason Home name. The Vasons created the formal boxwood garden on the property. (Photograph by Marcia Brooks.)

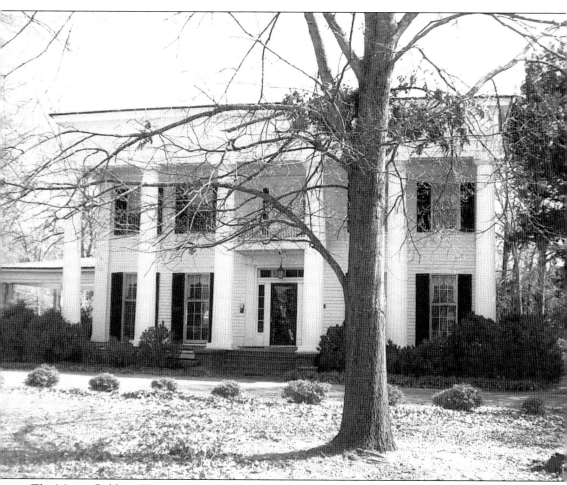

The Martin-Baldwin-Weaver House on North Main Street is a premier example of classic temple front Greek Revival architecture. Felix Martin built the home in 1850. It features Doric-order columns, a cantilevered balcony, and a typical Greek Revival entry with transom and sidelights. The home has been called the most significant "pure" example of Greek Revival architecture in Georgia. Frances Benjamin Johnston photographed it in 1919 as part of the Carnegie Survey of the Architecture of the South, which resides in the Library of Congress. The Baldwin family owned the home for a period of time. It was then purchased and restored by its current occupants, Russell and Dr. Rose Ann Weaver. All essential elements of the Greek Revival temple style of architecture are present, including Greek-order columns, geometrical ornamentation, and a flat roof style. (Photograph by Marcia Brooks.)

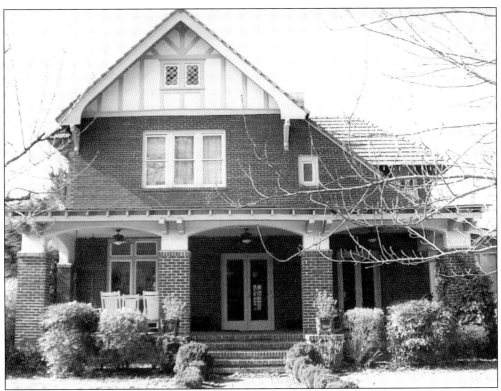

This Craftsman-style home on South Main Street was built around 1910. This style of architecture was popular throughout the early 20th century. Larger than many Craftsman bungalows, this home exhibits Tudor influences as well. This architectural style valued clean lines and attention to the patterns made by combining different building materials. (Photograph by Marcia Brooks.)

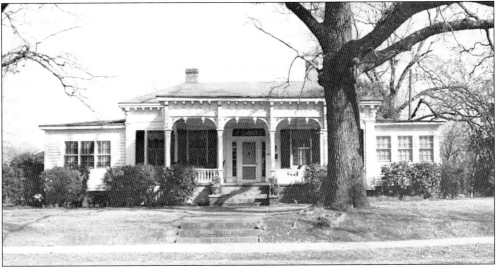

The Walton-Bearden-Chambers House on Eatonton Road at the southern end of the historic district was built in 1865. The home is an example of Eastlake-style ornamentation. It was used on various home styles of the Victorian period. This type of ornamentation is characterized by elaborate spindle work, as seen on the porch of this home. (Photograph by Marcia Brooks.)

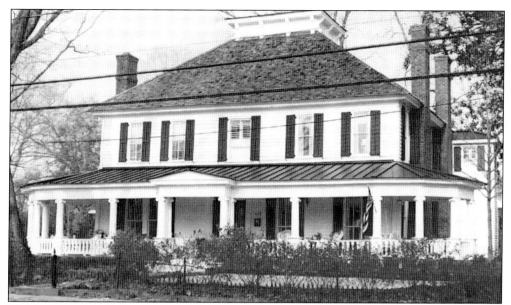

This home on South Main Street became the home of Paul and Lula Hurst Atkinson in the late 19th century. Paul eventually became the owner of three paintings depicting Civil War battles. These paintings were shown at the Cotton States Exhibition in 1895. Shortly thereafter, one painting was destroyed by fire and another by a tornado. The remaining painting was sold and later became a permanent fixture at the Cyclorama in Atlanta. (Photograph by Marcia Brooks.)

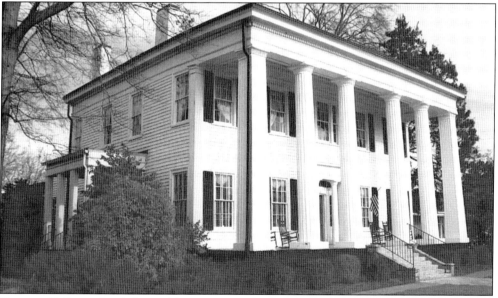

Heritage Hall is a Greek Revival home on South Main Street, open to the public for tours. It was built in 1811 by Lancelot Johnson and purchased in 1830 by Dr. Elijah Jones. In 1909, owner Stephen Turnell had the home picked up, placed on logs, and pulled by horses and mules to the current site to create space for the building of the First United Methodist Church. In 1977, the home was donated to the Morgan County Historical Society by Susan Reid Manley Law. Her grandmother, Sue Reid Walton Manley, was the last owner to live in it as a private residence. (Photograph by Marcia Brooks.)

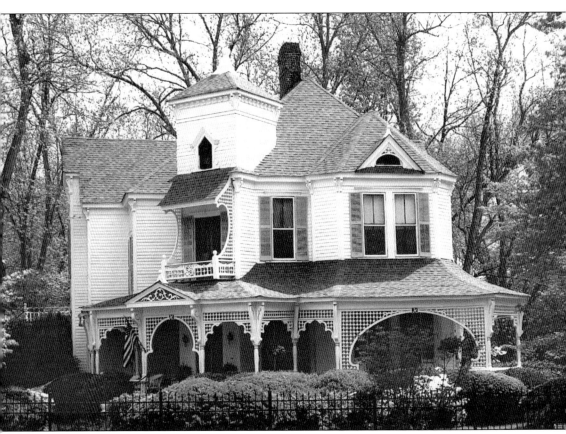

Hunter House is a Queen Anne–style home on South Main Street, built about 1883 by John Hudson Hunter. Hunter was a businessman who owned a drugstore in Madison. Later, he started Hunter Furniture Company. He was also one of the founders of the Bank of Madison. All of the millwork on the inside and outside of the home was handmade in Madison. Hunter House is acknowledged as the most photographed house in Madison. It was also the model for children's author Wylly Folk St. John's book *The Mystery of the Gingerbread House*. Locals still refer to it affectionately as "the Gingerbread House." The home has a hipped roof with cross gables and a square tower. The first- and second-story porches both have beaded and shaped spindle work. A pecan grove stands behind the house at the back of the property. (Photograph by Marcia Brooks.)

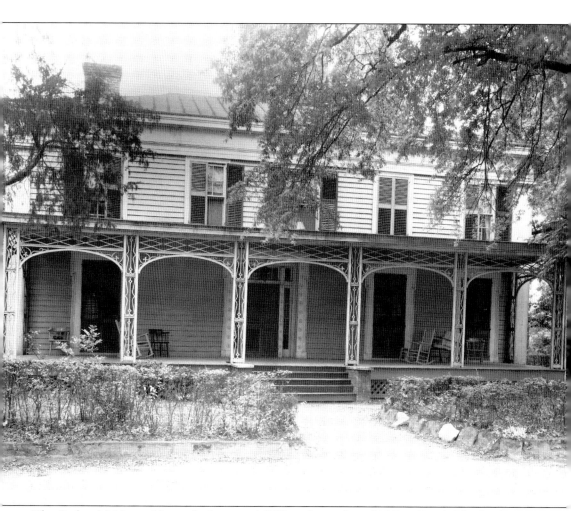

The Stokes-McHenry House, built around 1822, is located on Old Post Road. The land was obtained by a land lottery in 1820. Judge William Sanders Stokes originally built the house much smaller, just a basic double-pen cottage. It was considerably enlarged in 1840 and 1850. This late Federal Greek Revival–style house was occupied by descendants of the original owners for seven generations. The family maintained old manuscripts and first editions of books, along with original land deeds and other historic papers and items from the 18th, 19th, and 20th centuries. A traveler writing in the *New York Times* in 1997 spoke of the house containing canvas tents made for the Civil War and $12,000 in Confederate money that the children of the family have used for poker games for many years. Several of the bills are framed against black velvet. (Courtesy of the Library of Congress.)

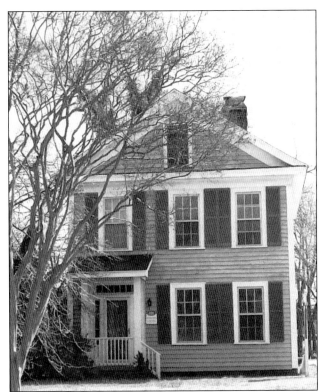

This beautiful and simple building, known as the Lockwood House, has been the office of Dr. Rose Ann Weaver for a number of years. It is located on North Main Street. The building is a Federal-style town house with an offset door and four symmetrical windows to the right of the door. It is not known when this building was constructed. (Photograph by Marcia Brooks.)

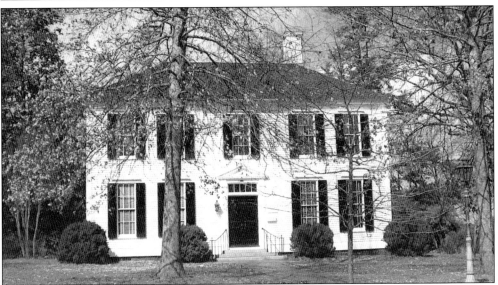

The Episcopal Parish House on Academy Street, also known as the Barnett Parish House, was built sometime between the 1840s and 1880s. Originally, the Madison Female Institute stood on this property. It was used as a Confederate hospital in 1864–1865 and later burned. The current structure may have incorporated remnants of the earlier building. Extensive exterior changes were made during the late Victorian era in the style of the time, but the home was returned to its original Federal facade when it was purchased as a parish house for the Episcopal Advent Church in 1965. (Photograph by Marcia Brooks.)

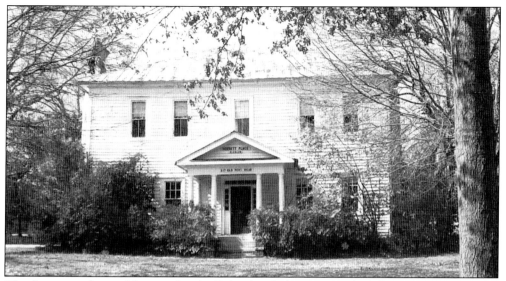

This house is a beautiful example of a Federal-style home typical of the Piedmont region of Georgia. Built in 1830, it is located on Old Post Road in Madison and most recently was operated as a bed and breakfast. Federal-style buildings have simple, clean lines and are often symmetrical. Several of Madison's early homes and businesses were constructed in this style. (Photograph by Marcia Brooks.)

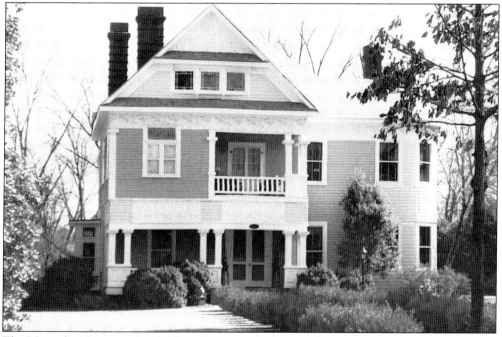

The Magnolia House on South Main Street was built around 1860. The Queen Anne structure served as the home for St. James Catholic Church for a period in the late 20th century before the church constructed a new building. While doing renovations prior to this time, a trap door was discovered that led to a tunnel that extended toward the Madison Presbyterian Church. It is thought that the tunnel may have been part of the Underground Railroad. (Photograph by Marcia Brooks.)

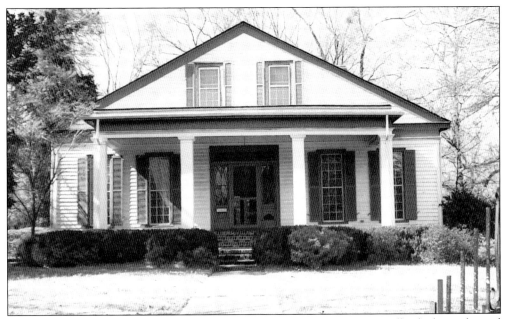

Pictured is the home of Dr. A.K. Bell, who was a Confederate surgeon. Originally, the home fronted on Old Post Road but now faces South Main Street. It was built in the first quarter of the 19th century. Many homes were used as military hospitals during the Civil War. Surgery at that time was very difficult, and many military men became amputees. Not a great deal of information is available on Dr. Bell. (Photograph by Marcia Brooks.)

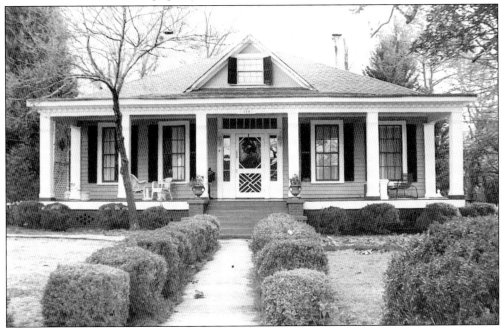

The Ivy Cottage on North Main Street is also known as the Evans-Jones House. It was built around 1853. This home was built in the early Classical Revival style, evidenced by its square columns and center pediment. Montpelier, the home of James Madison, is the national example of this architectural style. (Photograph by Marcia Brooks.)

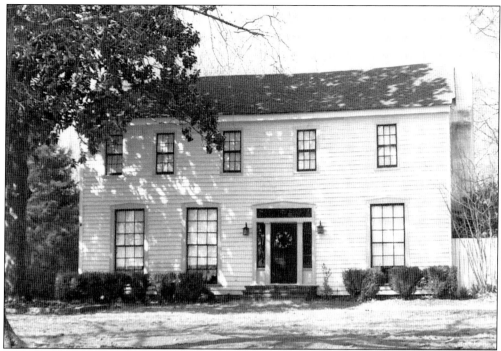

This home on North Second Street in Madison is known as the Saffold House. It was built in 1816 in the Piedmont Plain or Federal style. It was the home of Judge Adam Saffold, a circuit judge for the Morgan County vicinity, and his wife, Ann. The home was originally built with two rooms upstairs and two rooms downstairs and was later widened. (Photograph by Marcia Brooks.)

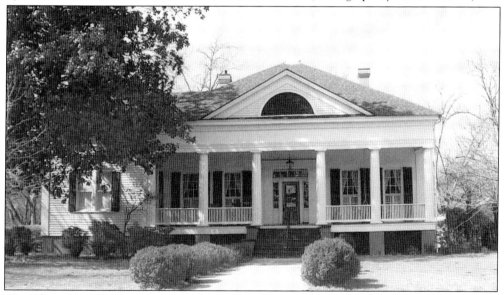

The Billups-Tuell House, also known as the Fears House, is located on North Main Street. This wood-frame variation on the classic raised Revival cottage was built in 1853. Its distinguishing characteristic is a unique and unusually large semicircular louvered arch on the front. Gen. Jeptha Vining Harris built the home in 1853 for his daughter Susan, who married Joel Abbot Billups. (Photograph by Marcia Brooks.)

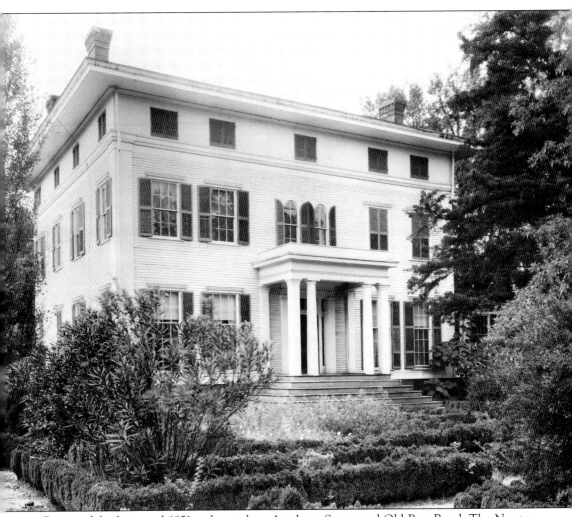

Boxwood, built around 1851, is located on Academy Street and Old Post Road. The Newton family has owned Boxwood since 1906. The back of the home, with an Italianate entrance, faces Academy Street, and the Greek Revival front entrance faces Old Post Road. Wilds and Nancy Kolb completed Boxwood in 1851. (Courtesy of the Library of Congress.)

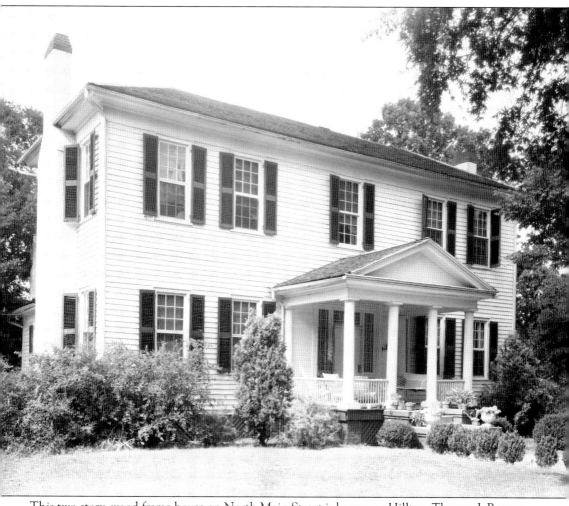

This two-story, wood-frame house on North Main Street is known as Hilltop. Thomas J. Burney built the home in 1838 for his bride. It was the lifelong home of Madison legislator E. Roy Lambert Jr. (1925–2008). His father, attorney Ezekiel Roy Lambert Sr., purchased the home in 1925. E. Roy Lambert Jr. opened his law office in Madison in 1950. The home is still owned by his widow, Chris Lambert. They have contributed a great deal to the development of the area. Among Chris's contributions, during her time on the library board, she was responsible for arranging for the Uncle Remus Regional Library Briar Patch Critters to be placed on the library grounds in Madison. These large sculptures, which pay homage to the characters in the tales of Georgia native Joel Chandler Harris, were once located at Lenox Square in Atlanta. When Lenox Square wanted to move them, they were acquired for the library in Madison through the efforts of Chris Lambert. (Courtesy of the Library of Congress.)

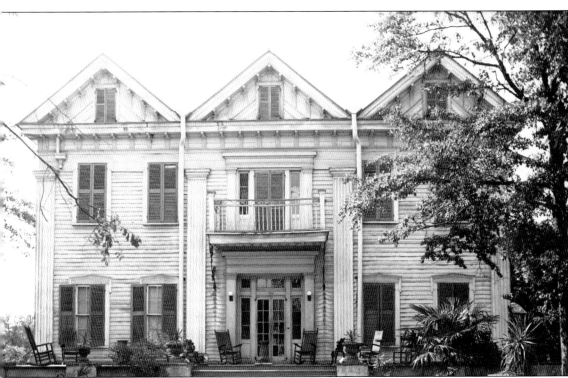

This home on Dixie Avenue is known as Thurleston, a reference to Thurleston Castle in Scotland from a poem by Sir Walter Scott. It is one of the most viewed homes in Georgia and has been visited by tourists from all over the world. In the 1980s, it was used in some early episodes of the television series *In the Heat of the Night*. The home was built about 1818 in the Plain architectural style. The original home was moved to this site by John Byne Walker in 1844. The front part of the home, with its English-type gables, was added by Dr. Elijah E. Jones in 1848, and the home was doubled in size. In 1863, the home was purchased by Col. David E. Butler. Butler served as president of the board of trustees of Mercer University and president of the Georgia Baptist Convention. (Courtesy of the Library of Congress.)

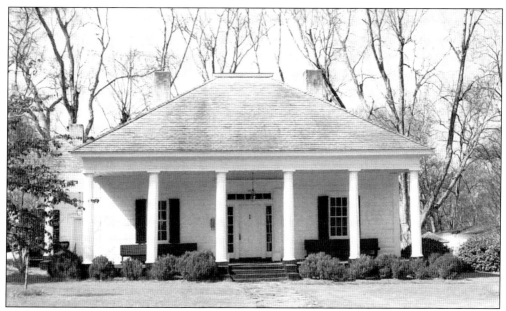

Nathan Massey built the Massey-Tipton-Bracewell home on North Main Street in 1854. Gen. Jeptha Vining Harris later purchased it. The house is a perfect example of a cottage built in the Greek Revival architectural style. It has been the home of Morgan County probate judge Mike Bracewell and his wife, Ruth, for a number of years. (Photograph by Marcia Brooks.)

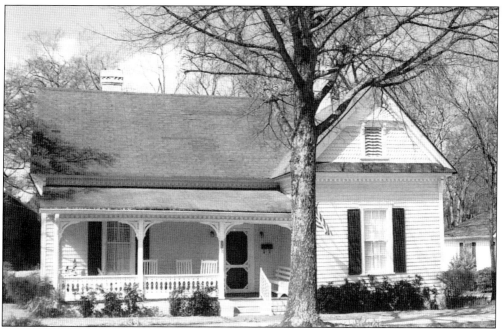

This home is next to the current location of Madison Drugs on North Main Street. Its basic style is the front-gable side-wing cottage. However, it incorporates Victorian details, such as the latticework. It also features an elaborate chimney. The front steps are unusual; the railing splits the steps into two separate entrances. (Photograph by Marcia Brooks.)

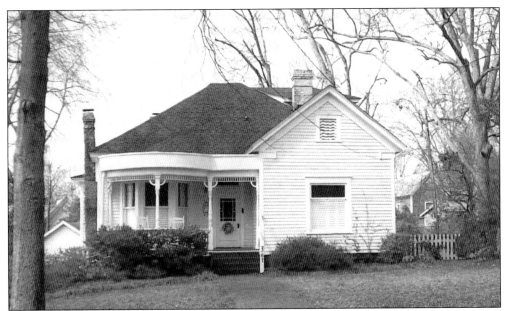

This home on North Main Street is similar to many other front-gable side-wing cottages in Madison. Its distinguishing feature, however, is its rounded porch. This styling, along with the latticework and plantation shutters, is reminiscent of Victorian-era details. Like so many other homes in Madison, this one is actually a blend of architectural styles. (Photograph by Marcia Brooks.)

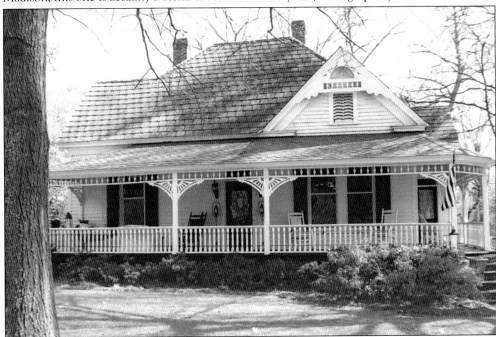

In this photograph is another home on North Main Street that has a basic front-gable side-wing design. However, its decorative features are even more like Victorian-style ornamentation. The home also has more nooks and crannies in the roofline than the typical front-gable side-wing design due to the hipped roof. The porch becomes semicircular on the right side, another Victorian feature. (Photograph by Marcia Brooks.)

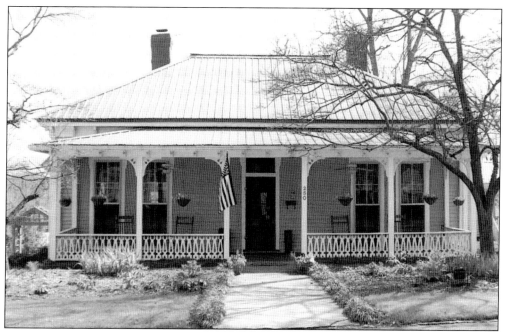

The Brady Inn is located on North Second Street. It operates currently as a bed and breakfast. The property actually consists of two homes integrated to provide accommodations to guests. The basic design of this home is faithfully Georgian; however, Victorian details have been added, such as the intricate latticework. (Photograph by Marcia Brooks.)

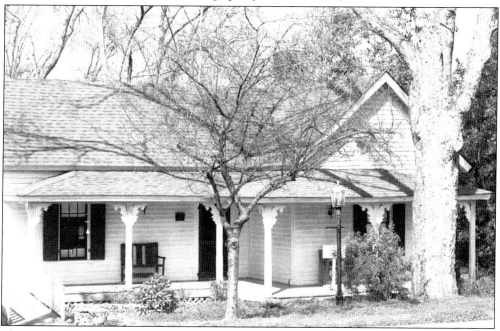

The Morgan County African American Museum opened in 1993. The small Victorian frame house, built about 1900, was donated by Alfred Murray and moved to the site. John Wesley Moore built the house. A farmhand, Moore was deeded about 41 acres of land from James A. Fanin on which to build the home. (Photograph by Marcia Brooks.)

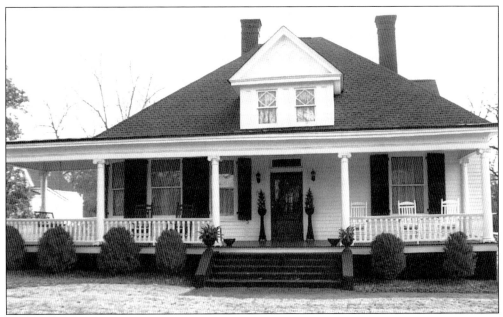

This house on North Main Street bears many features of Greek Revival architecture, such as its Doric columns. However, the home is more characteristic of the Free Classic style, which is distinguished by asymmetrical design, a complex roof system, and a porch. A centered dormer above the front porch adds to the Free Classic appearance. (Photograph by Marcia Brooks.)

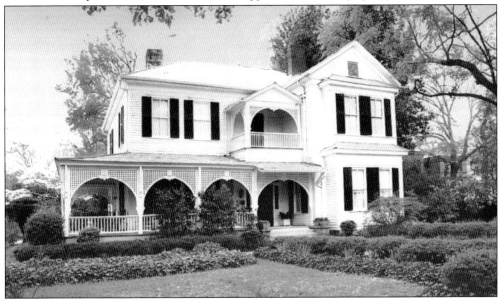

The Atkinson-Rhodes House is located next to the Madison-Morgan Cultural Center on South Main Street. Millard Filmore Atkinson built a one-story house on the site for his bride in 1893. In 1900, the home was enlarged and Queen Anne elements were added. Atkinson was a partner in Madison Variety Works, a company that produced intricate Victorian cutwork for homes. Many homes in Madison have cutwork produced by the company, including this one. Atkinson's daughter Martha was a music teacher at the Madison Graded School next door. (Courtesy of Marcia Brooks.)

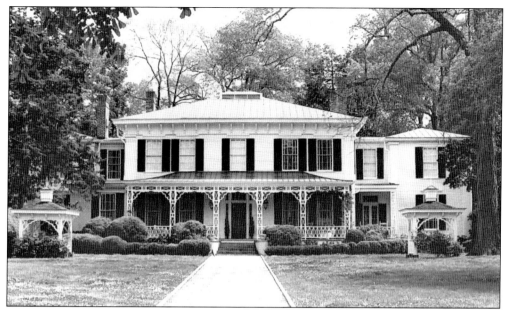

John A. Broughton acquired the Broughton-Sanders-Mason House, also known as Broughton Hall, in 1850. With entrances on Academy Street and Old Post Road, it includes original twin boxwood gardens. A 1950 tour of homes guide indicated that the gardens included one of the largest collections of azaleas and camellias in the country. The property remained in the family until it was sold to C.R. Mason in 1941. (Photograph by Marcia Brooks.)

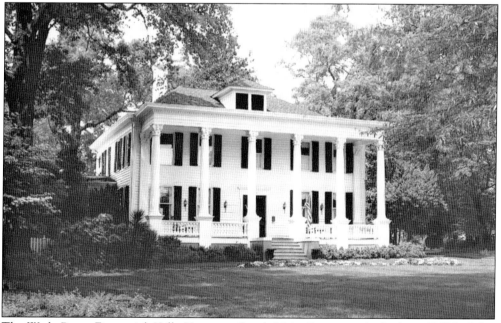

The Wade-Porter-Fitzpatrick-Kelly House on South Main Street was built about 1852 by John W. Porter and his wife, Mary Wade. Henry Harris Fitzpatrick, who bought the home in 1901, changed it extensively. He gave it a Classical Revival appearance and changed the South Main Street entrance to the main entrance. The home's original entrance was on South First Street, which later became Old Post Road. (Courtesy of Marcia Brooks.)

DISCOVER THOUSANDS OF LOCAL HISTORY BOOKS FEATURING MILLIONS OF VINTAGE IMAGES

Arcadia Publishing, the leading local history publisher in the United States, is committed to making history accessible and meaningful through publishing books that celebrate and preserve the heritage of America's people and places.

Find more books like this at
www.arcadiapublishing.com

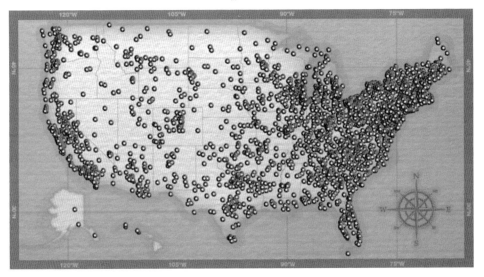

Search for your hometown history, your old stomping grounds, and even your favorite sports team.

 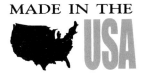